THE SUNDAY TIMES

WORLD LIBRARY

# RUSSIA

⑫

# ABOUT THIS BOOK

Charles W. Thayer began acquiring his special knowledge of Russia and its people when he served in the American Embassy in Moscow from 1933 to 1937. His experiences at that time, and in subsequent visits to the Soviet Union during his two decades in the foreign service, form the basis for this book. In 1953 Thayer resigned from the U.S. foreign service to take up full-time writing, and he has since become known both for his insight into Soviet policy and for his penetrating observations on the diplomatic world. His books include *Bears in the Caviar*, *The Unquiet Germans* and *Diplomat*.

THE SUNDAY TIMES WORLD LIBRARY

# RUSSIA

by Charles W. Thayer and the Editors of LIFE

THE SUNDAY TIMES · LONDON

# Contents

COVER: The Kremlin, left, Red Square and St. Basil's Cathedral beyond

# Introduction

This book on Russia, published by THE SUNDAY TIMES, is of tremendous interest because it presents in clear and readable form an introduction to Russia and its people. We who live in the West must learn to understand the leader of the Eastern group of nations—which is Russia, a vast country of over 200 million people. I have visited Moscow twice, first in 1947 during the Stalin regime, and secondly in 1959 to talk with Khrushchev. These visits enabled me to see something of the country from the air, and to observe the Russian people in the streets, and I was left with the impression that Khrushchev's Russia is very different from the days of Stalin. Today the people travel abroad and students visit Western centres of learning; a generation is growing up who want to know what life is like in the Western world, and their curiosity is boundless. For our part, we are learning that the great majority of the Russians are a friendly people at heart, particularly the peasants; they have suffered so much from internal oppression and external aggression that they long for the more abundant life in a peaceful world. But they have fears and suspicions about the West; their leaders encourage this mistrust, and by a strict Press censorship ensure that true information about Western life and intentions is put over in a distorted form—or withheld altogether.

In the West we suffer from certain disadvantages when trying to combat Communist pressure from the East; I will mention two. First, the East, by virtue of its ideology, places its fate in the minimum number of hands under strong and determined leadership; this makes it easier to formulate policy and announce decisions. In the West, we place our fate in the maximum number of hands and, among a group of nations, we find that national fervour makes it impossible to agree on a leader whom all will acknowledge and follow. Russia, because of its system, can concentrate her political, economic and scientific activities, and get her priorities right. In the West, because of our system and inability to agree on fundamentals, our efforts are dispersed; furthermore it is impossible to reach sound decisions, and "compromise" is the order of the day.

A second disadvantage is that in pursuance of the Communist aim of world domination, Russia used techniques which we would consider "ungentlemanly", and therefore do not use. The result is that we generally find we get the worst side of the contest. Perhaps we forget that the cold war is not in any way a gentlemanly affair, and we might do better if we occasionally took Russia on at her own game!

My own belief is that as the years pass the younger generation of Russians will become better educated; there will then develop a greater relaxation of tension in that country, and a less belligerent regime might eventually come to power—one which understands the context of the world in which it has to live—a younger generation with a longing for peace and the arts of learning. For this reason, we in the West must avoid the military aspects of what is commonly called "brinksmanship."

My final reflection on reading this book is that I am unable to agree with the conclusion in the final paragraph, which says:

"If you want peace, prepare for war."

A better slogan would be:

"If you want peace, *understand* war."

Today, war between East and West would be a nuclear war, which would have only one result— the destruction of Western civilization, and Eastern civilization too. This catastrophe must be avoided, if it is humanly possible to do so with honour.

We simply must find a way to "live and let live" with the East, led by Russia, avoiding all rigidity of thought, meeting the Russians more than halfway, visiting each other's countries,— while at the same time ensuring the overall security and vital interests of the Western world. It is surely better to negotiate than to threaten!

MONTGOMERY OF ALAMEIN
*Field Marshal*

# 1 Stage Setting

On a sunny day in Moscow a crowd pours out of Red Square between the Lenin Museum (left) and the Historical Museum.

# for a Stormy Empire

*In the background is the many-domed St. Basil's Cathedral*

IN its history, its size and its complexity, Russia is a world of its own. An American goes "over" to England or France. An Englishman goes "up" to London or "across" to Paris. But the visitor goes "in" to that sprawling land known as Russia but more correctly called the Soviet Union or the Union of Soviet Socialist Republics (U.S.S.R.). Yet were it not for the stern police and earnest Customs guards at the border it would be difficult to know just when you had entered the country. Eleven times in the past half-century the western frontiers of Russia—to use the land's traditional name—have shifted westward or eastward. Officially the frontier today is at Brest-Litovsk, the town where in 1918 the Bolsheviks made peace with the German Kaiser, but Soviet troops also stand guard on the River Elbe, 500 miles across Poland and Eastern Germany.

Nor will the landscape provide a clue even if you renounce the convenience of a plane for the slower but more revealing journey by railway. Some travellers say that Russia begins at Berlin's East Station, for once the outskirts of the city have been passed the countryside becomes flat and scrubby. Forests of birch trees alternate with meadows and cultivated fields. Instead of the neat, painted and compact villages typical of western Europe, straggling clusters of wooden houses appear along broad cobblestone roads. Instead of trim gardens, a few sunflowers adorn the front gardens. Chickens, geese and pigs are seen wandering nonchalantly about the muddy streets.

As you move further "in" through Poland the paint on the wooden huts fades until the log walls are bare and grey. The cultivated fields give way to swamps, and the birch forests, with their clusters of diminutive white-trunked trees, stretch interminably across the landscape. On and on the train rattles across the gently rolling countryside of European Russia (the country's western section), beyond the Pripet Marshes, where Russian armies have traditionally defended their frontiers against invaders from Europe—Swedes, Poles, Frenchmen and Germans.

OCCASIONALLY a provincial town appears on the horizon, shabby white, dominated by an onion-shaped church steeple whose once-gilded cross is rusted and bent or perhaps removed entirely if the church has been converted into a barn or a workers' club.

From time to time a tractor breaks the monotony of the motionless, featureless countryside, its plump girl driver wrapped in shawls so that only her fat red cheeks and wide eyes are visible. Perhaps a bearded, rubber-booted peasant prods a scrawny horse harnessed by a high yoke to a cart or sledge.

The unfenced fields and meadows of European Russia stretch to the distant horizon—and far beyond across the rich, rolling plains or "steppes" of the Ukraine to the Black Sea in the south, and across the endless forests and swamps to the Gulf of Finland and the Barents Sea in the north.

Only after long hours will the traveller see the first of the many rings that encircle Moscow, the Mecca not only of all Russians but of the entire Communist world. This circle is the *dacha* (villa) suburb where the important Muscovites maintain summer villas, while their poorer neighbours, unable to find a room in the city itself, live in dilapidated shacks.

In the distance are the high white spires of Stalin's skyscrapers, rising above the cupolas from which Moscow once got its name as "The City of Forty Times Forty Churches." Inside the White Russian station, the terminus from the west, you get your first pungent whiff of Russia: human sweat, the rancid smell of black bread, and mahorka—a cheap tobacco—burning in a cone made from a corner of the Communist newspaper *Pravda*. Every bench is crowded with shawled farm women and rubber-booted men, their bundles and boxes piled around them.

Presently you emerge on the wide black avenues which run in all directions from the Kremlin, strips of black asphalt often a hundred feet wide, jammed with open lorries spurting out black clouds of exhaust, droves of small taxis and a few shiny black limousines in which high officials sit beside the drivers to emphasize their democratic attitude. Many of the cars are old and dented and their paint is faded, but they are all clean, for it is forbidden to drive a dirty car through the streets of the Russian capital.

With disordered discipline the traffic charges ahead until a red light brings it to a grinding halt. A wave of pedestrians dashes across its path trying to reach the safety of the opposite pavement. Then with a roar of racing engines and a loud grinding of gears the lorries and cars leap forward as if from a race track's starting line.

ALONG the narrow pavements on either side of the avenue streams of pedestrians hurry to and from work, darting into shops to buy groceries or pausing for a few seconds to admire a window display. Their faces are stolid and expressionless, like those of any busy urban crowd. Most of the people are plainly but adequately dressed, the men generally in black or grey—for it shows the dirt less in a country where there are few good dry-cleaners. But many of the women seek more colour: print dresses, colourful scarves and hats in various shades from magenta to acquamarine.

The true Russians among them are distinguished by their round, flat faces, their high cheek-bones and wide eyes and their wide mouths which in moments of relaxation can stretch from ear to ear in laughter. But Moscow crowds are composed of many races. There are the lean, moustached, dark-eyed Georgians or Armenians, flat-faced Mongols from Kazakhstan, slit-eyed Chinese students, black visitors from Africa, and ascetic, thin, olive-skinned Indians.

Scurrying in and out of the crowds are groups of school children, the boys in blue-grey uniforms with peaked caps, and around their necks the red kerchief which is the insignia of the Pioneers, the Communist children's organization; the pigtailed girls in pinafores with clean white collars. Spotting a foreigner, the boys crowd around asking to exchange Russian coins or lapel badges for foreign ones. But if the uncomprehending foreigner thinks they are begging and tosses them some Russian money they will indignantly throw it back to him. Beggars are not seen on Moscow's streets. Only on the steps of churches are they to be found, tattered remnants of ancient Moscow—the Moscow of the czars and priests.

Though Moscow is indeed ancient, it is not the oldest city of Russia. That honour belongs to Kiev, now the provincial capital of the Ukraine but once the centre of an empire that reached almost beyond the Volga in the north-east. It was from Kiev that Russia's last pagan ruler, Vladimir, in the 10th century requested from the Patriarch of Constantinople that missionaries be sent out to convert his subjects to Christianity. The rulers of Kiev dominated Russia for almost 300 years, but at the end of the 12th century their leadership passed to princes in the north and eventually to the Muscovites.

MOSCOW itself was founded as a trading post in the 12th century. It remained a small village surrounded by a wooden palisade until Alexander Nevsky's son in the late 13th century unified the duchy of Muscovy, the nucleus from which the U.S.S.R. of today has grown. From then until the present day the city of Moscow has expanded in spasmodic leaps to keep pace with the empire of which it has been the centre—if not always the capital.

Here the old trade routes, the railways, the waterways and the lines of communication come together to form a giant nerve centre. From here originate the couriers of the Communist party, the telegrams and telephone calls, the newspapers and broadcasts which direct and guide the whole Communist empire.

The heart of Moscow is still the Kremlin. In the 15th century the old wooden stockade was replaced by the massive red brick wall which encloses the medieval fortress one sees today, a complex of palaces and churches in which Stalin and his successors have entertained political leaders from all over the world. It was in the ornate St. George's Hall that Stalin entertained representatives of the Western world coming to offer help after Hitler's invasion, while German bombers flew overhead.

OTHER palaces have been converted into assembly halls and government offices, a museum and a theatre. The old churches where once the czars of Russia were crowned, and where many of them lie buried, are now museums through which Soviet tourists reverently shuffle from tomb to tomb trying to decipher the names of their ancient rulers.

Just outside the walls is "old" Moscow—though few of its houses survived the great fire of 1812. Many are one-storey columned palaces designed in the Empire style by architects who were imported from Italy and France after the Napoleonic wars. Some are monumental post-revolutionary buildings housing Soviet Ministries. In the smaller side streets, huddled below Stalin's seven skyscrapers with their wedding-cake spires, are numberless little wooden houses, the plaster falling from their log walls and their chimneys leaning at precarious angles.

Further from the Kremlin and lining the great circular avenues built up in the Stalin era are the new ten- to fifteen-storey blocks of flats, their street facades ornate with balustrades, mosaics and pillars, their hidden rear walls a drab expanse of raw unplastered brick.

Finally on the outskirts of town where once collective farm cows grazed contentedly are the new residential communities built mostly since Stalin's day—massive cubes of unadorned pre-fabricated cement construction eight and ten storeys high where the upper classes are at last finding individual apartments of two or three rooms for themselves and their families.

As Moscow grew to be a great city, so ancient Muscovy grew to be the empire that is the U.S.S.R. today in waves of irresistible expansion followed by long periods of stagnation, foreign invasion and contraction. Among the first and most important of these invasions was that of the Tatars, a Mongolian people that dominated the country for more than 250 years until the end of the 15th century.

While the rest of Europe was undergoing the great changes of the Middle Ages and the Renaissance, Russia was held fast in the grip of these barbarians. Their highly-centralized despotism left its mark on Russian institutions and psychology long after Ivan the Great threw off the Tatar yoke in 1480 and set himself up as "Sovereign of All Russia." Even today Russia's most western cities, which escaped Tatar rule, retain a more European veneer and urbane aspect than their easterly counterparts.

The wave of expansion started by Ivan the Great continued under his son Vasily III and his grandson Ivan the Terrible, who advanced as far as the Baltic in the west, pushed the Tatars behind the Volga in the east and drove the Turks south to the Caspian Sea. But then the wave subsided, "The Time of Troubles" began, and soon the Poles overran the country. In 1610 they occupied Moscow.

A decade later the tide turned again and the Poles were hurled back to their own borders. A national assembly of nobles, merchants, clergy and soldiers met in 1613 and elected as their new czar Michael Romanov, the founder of a dynasty which was to rule Russia for more than 300 years until the Revolution. After another recession in the mid-17th century, a new surge added the eastern part of the Ukraine, until then an appendage of Poland, with its great fertile steppe—the gently rolling plains of south-western Russia.

Once again the wave fell back and this time in its wake came the Swedes who penetrated deep into Russian territory. But in 1707 Peter the Great, one of Russia's greatest rulers, rallied the country, evicted the invaders from the north and established his frontiers on the shores of the Baltic and the Gulf of Finland. Here on a swamp he had in 1703 begun construction of a new capital, St. Petersburg. Peter's new city was Russia's "Window on Europe." He not only brought Russia out of its own Dark Ages into the stream of European history but he forced Europe upon his reluctant countrymen, intro-

ducing Western concepts of administration, industry and warfare. Stripping his nobles of their oriental robes and clipping their long beards, he even forced them at the point of his dagger to look like Europeans.

Half a century later Catherine the Great advanced the western frontiers almost to the point they are today by moving into Poland and Lithuania. And like Peter, Catherine immersed the Russians in European concepts of literature, art and philosophy. But she punished anyone who resisted her rule as ruthlessly as did any of the old Tatar despots.

WHILE these great surges brought Russia to the west, other waves of expansion were rolling eastward to the shores of the Pacific, south eastward across the deserts of Central Asia to the foothills of the Himalayas and southward across the rugged Caucasus Mountains to the borders of Asia Minor.

The first of these eastward advances led across the Ural Mountains into Asiatic Russia or Siberia. From Moscow's eastern suburbs, a ribbon of cleared land nearly a hundred yards wide leads eastward across the Volga and over the Urals. This is the great Siberian *Tract*, Russia's centuries-old road to the Pacific.

Although it is asphalted in the vicinity of Moscow and cobblestoned in the neighbourhood of provincial cities, the Siberian *Tract* is for the most part a muddy, unpaved trail. As you follow it to the east you are treading in the footsteps of tens of thousands of exiles who since the 17th century have stumbled along it to work in the mines and forests of Siberia. Here and there are still visible the *etapes* or stations where the exiles and convicts camped overnight on their way to oblivion. In the forests and swamps on either side, only just a hundred miles from Moscow, bears, wolves, moose and deer roam the wilderness.

As it climbs the gentle western wooded slopes of the Ural Mountains the *Tract* leads past a cement obelisk which marks the dividing line between Asia and Europe. A few miles further comes Sverdlovsk, formerly Ekaterinburg, on the eastern slopes of the mountains. Here in 1918 the last of the czars was executed with his family when their Bolshevik guards panicked at the approach of anti-Bolshevik troops.

Sverdlovsk also boasts one of the world's greatest geological museums, a magnificent display case for the mineral wealth of the Ural area. As early as the 18th century the Ural mines had attracted the attention of Russia's rulers, who thereupon looked for labour to exploit them. In 1753 capital punishment had been abolished in Russia and in its place perpetual exile in Siberia was substituted. But then with the need for labour the list of offences punishable by Siberian exile steadily expanded and from year to year the dreary columns of prisoners stumbling along the great Siberian *Tract* grew larger and larger.

LONG after the czarist regime had disappeared the exile system was continued and expanded. While under the czars undesirables were frequently forced merely to reside in Siberia and even received pensions during their banishment, Stalin reduced their status virtually to that of slaves. Under him at least ten million were thought to have been sentenced to exile and forced to work not only in the mines but in the forests and other projects being built to provide a second industrial base behind the Urals. Many who survived their sentences were compelled to settle on the inhospitable land. Later Stalin's successor at last recognized that forced labour is unprofitable and eliminated the worst iniquities of the system. To replace convicts, the Kremlin has tried to recruit young settlers by the lure of high wages and special bonuses to work in the mines, the power projects and the factories being built in this remote area.

Beyond Sverdlovsk the *Tract* sweeps through great forests from which come most of Russia's timber. The opening of the Trans-Siberian railway in the late 19th century made it possible to move the raw timber to western markets. But until then Siberia had suffered from an almost fatal lack of effective transport.

BETWEEN the Urals and the Pacific, Siberia is cut by seven major rivers. But all of them flow north through the virgin forests of the Taiga into the frozen tundra and thence to the Arctic Ocean, which until recently was icebound for a large part of the year. The railway solved the problem of extracting the timber. Large-scale development of western Siberia began in 1930. And now the rivers are being exploited for hydroelectric power.

Until recently the area north of the Trans-Siberian railway was scarcely inhabited outside the camps of slave labour working the forests, the salt mines north of Irkutsk and the gold fields of the Lena River. During a day's journey down one of the major rivers one could expect to pass perhaps a single fishermen's village, its log cabins clinging to the banks of the swift, muddy, log-blocked river.

Here only bear, lynx, sable, and beaver provided veteran trappers with a livelihood. But today entire communities of new log houses are growing up to house the workers in the factories that are being built to utilize the new hydroelectric power.

South of the Siberian *Tract* and the Trans-Siberian railway are the beginnings of the Central Asian deserts: the dry plains of Kazakhstan where until a generation ago Mongol-featured nomads camped in their black tents and grazed their sheep on the sparse desert grasses. This is a bleak-looking country, treeless and seemingly waterless, though beneath the soil Soviet scientists have recently discovered gigantic underground lakes. In summer only the desert grasses hold the parched soil in place against 60-mile-an-hour winds. In winter the gales raise snow-drifts 50 feet high.

In 1955 thousands of Communist youth workers were sent by the Kremlin to the Kazakhstan plains to plough up the soil and plant wheat to supplement the Soviet Union's chronically short food supply. Today the giant state farms they built—wooden barns, barracks, sheds, schools and stores—occasionally break the monotony of the flat, sunbaked landscape.

The Siberian *Tract* ends at Irkutsk, but the Trans-Siberian railway continues on. Presently it comes to Lake Baikal, the deepest inland body of water in the world. Then it plunges on through the forests of larch and pine to the Amur River, which marks the border of Manchuria, and thence along the Amur in a giant bow to Vladivostok on the Pacific, 4,000 miles from Moscow.

Western Siberia, a land of more than five million square miles, had been claimed by no one and inhabited only by a handful of natives until the end of the 16th century, when a Russian adventurer, Ermak, claimed it for Muscovy. At the end of the 18th century Russian explorers and traders established a trading company in Alaska, with branches as far down the American coast as Fort Ross near San Francisco. But in 1867 the Russians sold to the United States their claims to Alaska and the eastern shores of the Pacific, and Russia's eastern-most frontier has remained at the Bering Strait ever since.

WHILE Catherine the Great's diplomats were pushing Poland's frontiers toward the west and freebooters were cutting their way across the Siberian wilderness, another great wave of Russian expansion headed southward across the Caucasus. As early as the reign of Ivan the Terrible, Cossack troops—mercenaries primarily from the Ukraine region—had reached the mouth of the Volga on the Caspian Sea. Today Astrakhan is a major fishing centre and a main source of the world's caviar. Due to evaporation and reduced drainage from the Volga River, the Caspian Sea is sinking at the rate of a few inches each year and the sprawling delta of the Volga is steadily reaching out into the shallow sea.

Peter the Great tried to push the frontier further south to Baku, then a part of Persia, but without success. Not until 1806 was the frontier advanced to Baku (one of the Soviet Union's principal oil sources). In 1828 it was placed at the Araks River, which flows into the Caspian near its southern end. Here the frontier has remained until this day despite efforts by Stalin to push it southward after the second World War.

WEST of Baku and bounded by mountains to the north and south lie the fertile, semitropical valleys of Georgia. They are famous for their wines and their fierce men, a leading

example of whom was Josef Stalin, the shoemaker's son and former seminary student who in 1924 clawed his way to the top of the Russian Communist Party and ruthlessly ruled the Soviet Union until his death in 1953.

Two centuries ago Georgia was a tiny Christian kingdom surrounded by hostile Moslem States and tribes. In 1783 it was granted status as a protectorate of Russia. Twenty years later it was still being hard pressed by the Turks in the south, and so it was incorporated into the Russian Empire.

Between Russia proper and Tbilisi, the cosmopolitan, almost western capital of Georgia, lie the rugged and spectacularly beautiful Caucasus Mountains stretching from the Caspian to the Black Sea and with snow-clad peaks as high as 18,000 feet.

The high mountain valleys are inhabited by fierce mountain tribes including the Chechen, Ingush and Kabardinians who for centuries resisted every attempt of the Russians to pacify them or interfere with their independent tribal life. In an effort to subdue their resistance and to improve access to Georgia the Imperial Government began in 1814 to build the famous Georgian Military Highway joining Tbilisi with the North. Even today, despite modern snowploughs, this spectacular road which clings to precipitous mountainsides and winds over high passes is often closed by snow for several months each year.

The road did provide access but it did not enable imperial troops to overcome the resistance of the tribes. Even after the Revolution, isolated in their valleys, they continued to resist attempts to "communize" them until the second World War. Then, when the Germans approached, they put themselves at the disposal of the invader against their historic foes, the Russians. But when the Germans were pushed back Stalin had his revenge. In a single day hundreds of thousands of the mountain people were rounded up, herded into cattle cars and shipped off to the plains of Kazakhstan. Not until Stalin was dead were the survivors allowed to return to their mountain home—defeated and dispirited relics of their ancient tradition.

THE last of the massive waves of Russian expansion before the second World War was directed south-east into Central Asia. Though the czars, particularly Peter the Great, had long dreamed of an overland route to India, the long desert belt called the Hungry Steppe, which separates Central Asia from Russia, discouraged him and his successors.

Not until 1865 did a Russian expeditionary force under the command of General Kaufmann set out for the Moslem town of Tashkent. A year later Tashkent was captured and it soon became the military headquarters from which further expeditions were sent to subdue the emirs of Samarkand, Bukhara, Khiva and Kokand. By 1884 the most remote of all the principalities, Merv, was captured and the borders of the Empire extended to the frontier of Afghanistan, where they have since remained.

Tashkent, the leading city and transport centre of the area, is one of the fast-developing cities in Russia. At its neat modern airport travellers from Indonesia, Burma, Malaya, Ceylon and India arrive wide-eyed and eager to see the wonders of modern Soviet industrialization, or depart laden with pamphlets and books on how to transplant the secrets of the Soviet system to their home countries.

Tashkent is really three separate cities: an old native quarter in which flat-roofed, whitewashed houses cluster together along narrow lanes, a European quarter dating from the first Russian occupation and containing wide shady streets and open squares bordered with one- and two-storey bungalows of Victorian design, and the New City, built under Soviet rule. In the latter an ornate new opera house faces on an enormous square typical of the Stalin period of city planning.

The square is a favourite spot for citizens to sit while enjoying the cooling breezes from the water of a tremendous fountain whose spouts send up jets of water 20 and 30 feet into the air. Across the square is the city's imposing new hotel, gleaming white and adorned with Persian arches and alabaster filigree.

AT one corner of the hotel is an outdoor "shashlik" restaurant where the smell of mutton roasting on a charcoal grill reminds you that you are in the very heart of Central Asia. Around the tables sit Uzbeks, small wiry men, their eastern faces brown and wrinkled, wisps of beards dangling from their chins, their short cropped heads covered with brightly coloured skull caps. Over their shoulders they wear long silk or cotton *khalats* (gowns) dyed in stripes of mauves and reds and yellows.

Not far from the main square is a shopping area built chiefly before the Revolution. Here Uzbeks, Kazakhs and Tadzhiks from the outlying towns and villages come to buy the small luxuries their local shops do not stock: ready-made suits, dresses and, above all, shoes. The European visitor must push and elbow his way through excited but good-natured crowds to get to the counter to buy himself the straw hat he will certainly need to protect himself against the glaring Central Asian sun.

Tashkent lies in the centre of a well-watered oasis. Today the fields are consolidated into giant farms which supply the Soviet Union with most of its cotton.

An hour away from Tashkent by air, or 24 hours in a wooden-benched third-class train, is the ancient capital of all Central Asia, Samarkand, one of the oldest cities in the world. Samarkand has a bazaar where traders and farmers sit cross-legged in their booths, surrounded by their

| PEOPLES OF THE SOVIET UNION: | |
|---|---|
| Russians | 114,588,000 |
| Ukrainians | 36,981,000 |
| Belorussians | 7,829,000 |
| Uzbeks | 6,004,000 |
| Tatars | 4,969,000 |
| Kazakhs | 3,581,000 |
| Azerbaijanians | 2,929,000 |
| Armenians | 2,787,000 |
| Georgians | 2,650,000 |
| Lithuanians | 2,326,000 |
| Jews | 2,268,000 |
| Moldavians | 2,214,000 |
| 113 Others | 19,701,000 |
| Total | 208,827,000 |

wares: round flat discs of unleavened bread, a dozen varieties of melons, jars of saffron, curry powder and a dozen more herbs whose pungent smells fill the air.

Samarkand also has a modern shopping street where State-owned stores sell perfume from Moscow, shoes from Czechoslovakia and toys from Eastern Germany. But even for Soviet officials Samarkand's greatest boasts are the mosques and Moslem seminaries of the ancient civilization of Tamerlane, who himself lies buried in a beautiful blue-tiled tomb in the heart of the town.

WHAT kind of people occupy this sprawling empire? Few generalizations can apply to a conglomeration of peoples who speak a hundred languages and dialects and whose racial and cultural origins spring from a score of civilizations from ancient Greece to Genghis Khan's Mongolia. What can the Moscow intellectual whose forefathers debated with Goethe and Voltaire have in common with a Prime Minister of Kazakhstan who was born in a nomad camp the son of a Mongolian shepherd?

Despite the intermingling of the many neighbouring races, the Russians have continued to dominate the country. In Tbilisi, Tashkent and Alma-Ata the figureheads of local government may be Georgians, Uzbeks or Kazakhs, but the tough party bosses behind the scenes are most frequently descendants of the colonizers and conquerors. They are bullet-headed Russians from Moscow or Leningrad.

ESSENTIALLY the inhabitants of the U.S.S.R. are a primitive people in the sense that they have not yet been sophisticated by cosmopolitan life, softened by modern comforts or confused by the plethora of choices that are available in a highly developed community. Like their land, their thoughts and ideas are large, plain and open.

Behind their hard exteriors one can detect in them traces of their turbulent history: the fatalism inherited from their traditional Orthodox religion, the suspicion and fear of foreigners which derives from their acute awareness of the vulnerability of their frontiers.

Toward those who have aroused their ire the Russians can be implacable, as anyone can attest who has seen them marching into action against an enemy—endless solid ranks doggedly advancing. The whine of dive bombers, the crash of artillery and the chatter of machine guns may have told them that directly ahead lies a narrow defile or perhaps a tottering bridge which they must pass if they are to survive. Below their low-slung helmets their faces are almost inhumanly stolid and from deep in their throats comes a low, defiant, almost religious battle song promising death to their enemies and victory for their fatherland.

But left alone the Russians can be a friendly people. Cut off throughout their history from the outside world, they are intensely curious about life beyond their national horizons and when their fears and suspicions are allayed they are both amicable and hospitable to foreign visitors.

*Shrouded in the haze of winter, the domes of St. Andrew's Church overlook Kiev, Russia's capital centuries ago*

# Vast and Varied Domain

Russia is a country in which a feeling of remoteness, gigantic in scope and endless in time, seems to dwarf mortal man. This is true not only in the icicled chill of the aged city of Kiev (*above*) but, as the following pages will show, in European Russia's Volga River basin, in Soviet Central Asia and in Siberia. The vast and lonely land nurtures a dark sense of unreality and serves as a natural backdrop for recurrent excitement, drama and violence. It also challenges the efforts of modern leaders to bring about a long-awaited modernization.

IN GORKY, on the Volga River, two children visit the city's ancient showpiece, a tall 14th-century "kremlin," or fortress, whose wall and tower dominate the river port.

EUROPEAN RUSSIA *has a strong visual and cultural affinity with the West. Its people, mostly Slavic, dominate the rest of the U.S.S.R.*

ALONG THE VOLGA, the main artery of western Russia, a two-way traffic of barges moves at sunset.

IN THE UKRAINE, granary of the U.S.S.R., a lone peasant drives out to collect firewood.

## A CAPITAL TRANSFORMED *by winter's magic,*
*Moscow in the snow becomes a city of cold, strange beauty*

FESTIVE TROIKAS, bright with colour, glide along a snowy road on the city's outskirts, heading for the sport in Izmailovsky Park.

GLOOMY RED SQUARE is touched by the wan glow of a low morning sun. Street lights are kept on to cheer people on their way to work.

# GEORGIA *is a wild land of rugged mountains which have long sheltered fierce men*

TOWERING DICTATOR, a 33-ton copper statue of the Georgian Josef Stalin looks out on Stalingrad. Stalin's successor Khrushchev denounced the figure as wasteful.

TOWERING MOUNTAINS, with tilled fields on their steep foothills, helped the Georgians for centuries to repel invaders. A few tough horsemen, like the rider picking his way through the shallows of the river (*bottom*), could hold a pass against an entire army, and thus Georgian tribes long stayed free of czarist attempts to subdue them.

IN THE KIRGIZ RANGE in Soviet Central Asia a shepherd drives his sheep up from their wintering on a lower
slope. The sheep are the property of the Soviet State. The
people of Soviet Central Asia, while stubbornly individu-
alistic by tradition, have profited greatly in recent years
from modern farming methods introduced by the State.

16

SOVIET CENTRAL ASIA, *largely a cotton-growing area, has been predominantly Islamic for centuries. There are some 26 million Moslems and former Moslems in the Soviet Union*

CARAVAN OF HAY makes its way across the steppe near the city of Bukhara. The vanquished emirs of ancient Bukhara were notorious for their cruelty.

AGED DRIVER of a heavily laden wagon between Alma-Ata and Frunze is a picturesque remnant of an Asian civilization that is gradually disappearing.

SIBERIA *evokes the image of merciless wastes populated only by political exiles. Actually the land holds infinite promise—and the Russians are developing it confidently*

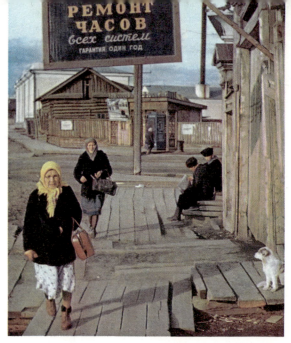

**PLANK PAVEMENT,** the only kind that the Siberian city of Yakutsk has to offer, is trudged by shoppers. Above it a watch repairer's sign says his work is guaranteed.

LONELY CEMETERY outside Yakutsk has protective fences set around new graves. Older graves are slightly raised because the deep frost forces objects to the surface.

LOG ROAD, characteristic of Siberia, is repaired by men and women who fit together sawed-timber sections. These last only eight years because of Siberia's endless frost.

# 2

# The Rise of the Communist State

THE expansion which over the years pushed Russia's frontiers constantly forward was until 40 years ago the product of three basic forces: the restlessness of Russia's virile population, the people's fear of being crushed by their neighbours, and plain human covetousness. Perhaps, too, the drive was spurred on by the curiosity that impels the inhabitants of a rolling plain to push on to the top of the next rise just to see what is on the other side.

But in this century a dynamic new element was added to these age-old compulsions, making Russian expansionism a challenge not just to her neighbours but to the entire world. That element was international Communism.

The father of Communism, Karl Marx, once predicted that countries more advanced industrially than Russia would be earlier in adopting the cure he so fanatically recommended for the world's ills. As in so many of his other predictions he turned out to be wrong. Why? The answer is perhaps a dual one: the peculiarly distressing ills caused by czarism, and a man named Lenin.

The cruel autocratic rule of the czars was a heritage partly of the Mongol khans and partly of the Byzantine Empire which had flourished to the south. For centuries it was personified by tyrannical landlords, corrupt tax collectors, brutal conscription officers, bigoted Orthodox priests and finally the monstrous bureaucracy which enforced the laws tying the peasants to the soil as serfs or virtual slaves.

AS early as 1773, during the reign of Catherine the Great, a widespread revolt broke out under the leadership of a Cossack named Emelyan Pugachev. Its chief grievances were the harsh rules of military service, the injustices of serfdom and the Church's suppression of religious freedom. The revolt was suppressed but the grievances remained and continued throughout the first half of the 19th century to stir up sporadic outbursts of peasant violence.

In 1790 a Russian intellectual named Alexander Radishchev, who wrote a pamphlet denouncing the iniquities of the landlords and bureaucrats, was arrested and banished to Siberia—one of the first of many thousands of political exiles to be sent beyond the Urals.

In December 1825 a small group of reformers, inspired by Western experiments in constitutional government, attempted to stage an uprising. But this, too, was suppressed.

With the tension mounting, Alexander II, a czar with more realistic views than his predecessors, came to the imperial throne in 1855. Acknowledging the necessity for reform, he took the first big step by liberating the serfs. But other desperately needed reforms were slow in coming. After Alexander was assassinated in 1881 by a terrorist group another wave of reaction set in.

But unrest was steadily growing in the countryside. Organized bands of peasants raided the mansions of local landlords, burning their records, confiscating their grain and carrying off their farm implements, while the unfortunate owners could only stand by helpless.

In St. Petersburg and Moscow a growing army of workers, attracted from the farms by the first surge of Russian industrialization, was stirring restlessly. The first big break came in 1905. An extraordinarily vital and able priest, Father Georgy Gapon, had organized a society of industrial workers in St. Petersburg. Gapon advocated reform through mass appeal to the czar himself, Nicholas II. On a cold January Sunday, Gapon's followers formed a giant procession and marched to the Winter Palace, singing "God Save the Czar," to present a peaceful petition for relief from their oppressive conditions.

A panicky officer ordered the czar's troops to fire and a sheet of bullets poured into the solid mass of humans. Hundreds were mowed down, their portraits of the czar and crosses falling with them. "Bloody Sunday" was the last organized attempt to win reforms by appeal.

IN the autumn of that year factory workers staged a general strike in St. Petersburg and organized themselves into *soviets* or councils. This was the high point of the "1905 Revolution" and it so frightened Nicholas that he acceded to the formation of a legislative body by election. But the Duma, as the resulting parliament was called, was strictly limited in power and dominated by a restricted electorate. While moderate political parties continued to operate in the open, the more revolutionary organizations flourished underground, fanning the smouldering resentment of all but a tiny section of aristocrats and landlords. Finally the reverses of the first World War ignited the inflammable substructure and set the entire ramshackle system in flames.

The immediate causes of the conflagration were readily apparent. Both the army and the home front were disillusioned by defeats; severe economic shortages were gripping the hinterland; the cumbersome czarist bureaucracy was hopelessly unable to cope with its problems; and finally there were scandals in the imperial palace itself, instigated by a dissolute, self-appointed holy man, Grigory Rasputin, whose hypnotic influence over the czarina paralyzed the court just when action was most needed to rescue the regime.

Discontent among workers, soldiers, generals and politicians reached the breaking point in February (March by the Western calendar) 1917. Organizing themselves into a *soviet*, the industrial workers of Petrograd (as St. Petersburg had been renamed during the war) were shouting for reform. In a few days they were joined by soldiers. In the Duma political leaders demanded the formation of a responsible Cabinet to end the governmental chaos.

NICHOLAS II, a kindly but stupid man imbued with his absolute autocracy, had up to then ignored all warnings. When the Duma president sent him a plea for concessions, Nicholas commented: "This fat Rodzianko has written me some nonsense to which I will not even reply." Instead he ordered the Duma to be dispersed.

But the Duma refused and with the approval of delegates from the Petrograd Council of Workers' and Soldiers' Deputies (called the Petrograd Soviet for short) it formed a provisional government and promised a constituent assembly to draft the long-sought constitution. The czar replied by ordering his troops to suppress the revolutionary government, but the generals were already pledging their support to it. At last, with no other choice, Nicholas abdicated. The czarist regime was not pushed out or supplanted. It simply collapsed.

The provisional government ushered in by the so-called February Revolution was a moderate one and included representatives of the Duma and the Petrograd Soviet. It was headed by a somewhat colourless liberal, Prince Lvov, and its chief link with the more radical Soviet was Alexander Kerensky, by far the most energetic member of the Cabinet.

The provisional government soon found itself facing incredibly difficult problems. On the military front resistance was dwindling. Behind the front there were severe shortages. The manufacture of war supplies had dropped off, and there was growing unrest among peasants and workers. Morale was a low ebb and the cry for peace and bread was growing.

But at this point another factor which was destined to transform the entire Revolution entered the situation. Its roots had been planted some seventy years earlier when a brilliant and bitter German economist and revolutionary named Karl Marx proclaimed Communism the key to the future. Working in the British Museum, he had evolved an elaborate "scientific" justification of the inevitability of Communism to be achieved through class struggle. He claimed a universal application of his theory and programme, saying that it would wipe out all economic and political injustice from all systems of government for all time.

Marx's system envisaged the abolition of private ownership by violent proletarian revolution, the gradual withering away of national States and a universal order based on a simple principle: "From each according to his ability; to each according to his needs." This system, Marx insisted, would displace capitalism everywhere and spread throughout the world.

Marx's Communist Manifesto, proclaiming the inevitable doom of capitalism, had been published in 1848. In the next generation it had won many disciples throughout Europe, among them a group of Russian revolutionaries who in 1898 had formed the Russian Social Democratic party. The latter openly espoused the Communist programme.

AMONG its adherents was a provincial Russian intellectual, Vladimir Ilich Lenin. A short, nervous, intensely single-minded man and an ardent Marxist, Lenin was, above all, a genius in the field of political tactics. Disgusted with the "go-slow" tactics of moderate Russian revolutionaries, he insisted that his party become a tightly-organized band of conspirators.

"Lenin," wrote Maxim Gorky, the Communist writer, "was a man who prevented people from leading their accustomed lives as no one before him was able to do." His insistence on selfless discipline, the keystone to his eventual success, was resisted among Social Democrats. In 1903 the party split. One part, the alleged majority or "Bolsheviks" (the word comes from the term for "majority," though actually they were a minority), sided with Lenin. The others, the "Mensheviks" or minority, rejected his demands for a completely totalitarian party.

After exile in Siberia and a stay in western Europe Lenin returned to Russia in 1905 but fled once more in 1907 to remain abroad, travelling about and finally ending in Switzerland. He was generally recognized as the most radical leader of the revolutionary movement.

WHEN the moderate February revolution ended czarism in 1917, its leaders announced their determination to continue the war against Germany. The Bolsheviks on the other hand had denounced all "imperialist wars" and demanded peace. Soon after the German government, suspecting that Lenin's presence in Petrograd might accelerate the popular agitation to take Russia out of the war, offered him safe conduct in a sealed train across Germany, whence he made his way to Petrograd.

There he immediately took charge of the Bolsheviks, who had been vacillating between co-operating with the provisional government and fighting it. Stepping up the party's propaganda activities and agitation among the troops of the city's garrison, he manoeuvered to get his men in control of the Petrograd Soviet.

As the provisional government sought in vain to win the loyalty of the army, Lenin saw the moment approaching for a strike. "To delay is a crime!" he shouted at his supporters, insisting that the Bolsheviks should seize power at once. Convinced by his driving energy and self-assurance, they redoubled their efforts to win over the troops in Petrograd. Little by little the regiments of the city's garrison were persuaded either to come over to the Bolsheviks or at least to remain neutral.

Finally Lenin decided to strike on October 25. "October 24 was too early," he told his uncertain followers. "October 26 will be too late." Early that morning from his headquarters in a girls' school he proclaimed the slogan "All power to the soviets"—the councils of workers and soldiers which he now calculated he could dominate. Then he ordered his Bolshevik bands and army supporters to take over all government buildings, including the Winter Palace, where Kerensky, the head of the provisional government since Lvov's resignation in August, and his Cabinet were desperately trying to rally loyal troops to defend themselves.

Faced by mounting mutiny, Kerensky slipped out of the city, hoping to rally troops at the front to march on the capital and throw out the Bolsheviks. But even the High Command was deaf to his pleas. Before he could return to the capital Petrograd had fallen into Lenin's hands. Within a few days the disciplined Communist conspirators posted in Russia's principal cities took over the local governments. The October Revolution, to the amazement of the world—including many Communists—was an accomplished fact.

It was a bloodless revolution; few lives had been lost.

AMONG the first acts of the triumphant revolutionaries was the abolition of all private land holding. Soon afterwards a telegram was sent to the German army High Command asking for an armistice. The Germans agreed to negotiate, and some weeks later Lenin's chief aide, the Jewish intellectual Leon Trotsky, led a peace delegation to Brest-Litovsk. From Trotsky's train as he arrived, pamphlets were scattered calling upon German troops to revolt. Throughout the negotiations which led to a peace treaty in 1918 it was obvious that Trotsky was playing for time for the pamphlets to take effect and to set off the revolution he hoped for in Germany.

On the day after the Revolution Trotsky had declaimed: "There are only two alternatives: either the Russian Revolution will create a revolution in Europe or the European Powers will destroy the Russian Revolution."

Trotsky was wrong on both counts. But in the three-year civil war which followed the Revolution the European Powers did come within a stroke of defeating the Bolsheviks' Red Army, which had been hastily organized by Trotsky. Anti-Bolshevik or "White Russian" troops attacked from every quarter and were supported by allied troops: French groups in Odessa, a

British expeditionary force in the Trans-Caucasus and in Archangel and Japanese troops in Siberia. American troops also participated.

All these attacks were repulsed, but not until the revived Polish State, which had attacked in the west, had been turned back were the last White armies driven from Russian soil. By the end of 1920 the civil war was over and the Communists were masters of Russia.

Four things prevented the defeat of what was originally a pitifully weak Bolshevik government: the divided leadership of the White Russian troops; the failure of the White Russians to arouse popular backing; growing Russian suspicion of all foreign intervention; and finally the Red Army's strategic position at the core of the country's transport network.

EVEN while the White and foreign troops were trying to upset the Soviet regime, the Communists hoped that the proletarian uprising so confidently predicted by Lenin and Trotsky during the first days of the October Revolution would somehow take place in western Europe. In 1919 the Communist International or "Comintern" was organized to aid these hoped-for revolutions. A revolt did occur in 1919 in Berlin, and Communist regimes held power for brief periods in Bavaria, Hungary and other areas. But as the new governments of western and central Europe regained stability Communist uprisings ceased.

Indeed a new kind of revolt now occurred. In February 1921 sailors at Kronstadt, a naval base guarding Petrograd harbour, struck briefly against the Communist rule. At the same time there were peasant uprisings.

These revolts were symptoms of the disorganization and discontent which had engulfed Russia. The civil war had left the country starving, its factories scarcely operating, its peasants refusing to part with their food to feed the cities. More than a million workers had deserted their factories and returned to the rural villages. In 1921–1922 a severe famine caused great loss of life in several rich agricultural areas. Lenin was forced into a major economic retreat.

EMBARKING on a New Economic Policy (NEP) in 1921, the Communist government relaxed its earlier measures to establish Communism and once again permitted the re-establishment of private trade and small-scale private industry. The economy rapidly revived.

Abroad, too, the Communists faced setbacks. The much-awaited world revolution had failed to materialize. Here again Lenin called for a retreat and instructed the Communist parties abroad to co-operate with other left-wing parties. Instead of trying to overthrow governments, they were to enter the ranks of trade unions so as to establish their leadership of the working class. The ultimate purpose was to use this leadership to foment revolution when times might be more propitious.

In 1922 Lenin became seriously ill. Now a new figure, a gruff and wily Georgian named Josef Stalin, came to the fore. Still a relatively unknown party leader, Stalin began his long compaign to oust Trotsky as second-in-command and heir presumptive to Lenin. Many issues divided Stalin the conspirator from Trotsky the intellectual, but the most important of these was undoubtedly the matter of world revolution. Trotsky still expected early revolutions in other countries, especially in Germany, and felt that Russia should work to bring these about as they would be of great assistance in establishing the Socialist system in Russia.

Stalin on the contrary maintained that it was quite possible to establish "Socialism in one country" simply by reconstructing the internal economy. Stalin won the fight partly because he was shrewder and more ruthless. But his programme also implied greater confidence in Russia's strength, and was therefore more popular with the party membership.

Finally, Trotsky was banished and Stalin in 1927 became the dictator of Russia, a role he was not to relinquish until his death in 1953.

BY proclaiming his intention of building Socialism in one country, Stalin did not mean to abandon the Communist dream of world revolution. It was rather a question of emphasis.

The industrialization of Russia came first; attempts to stir revolution came second.

Forced by the necessity of securing foreign credits and persuading Western technicians to assist his industrialization drive, beset by peasant resistance to his agricultural reforms, and obsessed by fears of opposition from Old Bolsheviks, Stalin consistently subordinated his interest in Communist parties abroad to his immediate aim of strengthening Russia. At the same time he told the Comintern to continue fighting political moderates in other countries.

In the early 1930s, rather than permit a left-wing, anti-Communist government in Germany, Stalin ordered the German Communists to side with the Nazis against the moderate left, thus giving Hitler a considerable boost in his rise to power.

In 1934, alarmed now by Hitler's anti-Russian pronouncements, the Soviet Union joined the League of Nations. A year later it concluded an alliance with France. In 1936 Stalin permitted the French Communist party to support the hitherto despised Socialists in forming a French Popular Front government under Leon Blum.

The outbreak of the Spanish Civil War in the same year, however, presented Stalin with a dilemma. On the one hand, the existence of Fascist regimes in Italy and Germany held a threat, for a Fascist victory in Spain might help bring about a right-wing coalition against him in Europe. Yet military aid involved sending Soviet personnel through other countries where more idealistic revolutionaries might "contaminate" them. Stalin vacillated. At first he permitted all-out military intervention with Soviet technicians and advisers and international brigades. Then, changing course, he ordered his officers home.

When the Western Powers at Munich in 1938 gave the Sudetenland to Germany without consulting Russia, they effectively drove Stalin into Hitler's arms. Later, negotiations for an alliance between Russia and the West came to naught and in 1939 Stalin surprised the world by signing a non-aggression pact with Hitler. The two dictators agreed to split Poland and the rest of eastern Europe between them, thereby assuring Hitler

peace on the eastern frontier while he attacked France and Belgium.

That this involved a sudden and radical switch of policy for the Western Communist parties did not disturb Stalin. His sole aim was to gain time to create an industrial base in Russia with which he might defend "the citadel of Communism," and whence, after the Western antagonists had bled themselves white, he might launch the final crusade for world Communism.

BUT on June 22, 1941, early strollers in Moscow's streets were startled by a solemn voice over the loudspeakers mounted at every corner: "Attention! Citizens! Shortly you will hear an important government announcement." After several hours they heard the shaky voice of the Foreign Minister, Molotov, telling them of the surprise attack launched against them by Germany. Molotov's tone was strikingly apologetic —and with good reason. Stalin had told his subjects that his agreement with Hitler meant that the war would be kept from Russia's frontiers.

Twelve days later Stalin himself broadcast. He appealed to his people to resist, in the name not of Communism but of country. This was no ideological war, where the sympathies of his people might be divided. This was a patriotic war to defend Russian soil. It was an appeal that throughout Russian history has seldom gone unanswered.

Then followed the initial German advance to the gates of Moscow, then the second Nazi drive to the Volga; the resistance at Stalingrad. Finally the tide turned and the Russian armies advanced slowly and relentlessly through Poland, Rumania, Germany and Austria to Berlin and Vienna, ultimately meeting the Western Allies on the Elbe.

WITHIN a month of the attack by Hitler Britain and the United States, recognizing that Nazi Germany was the most imminent menace, had pledged their support to the Russian forces, and during the course of hostilities they had shipped millions of pounds' worth of munitions, equipment and food to the Soviet Union.

After the war, at Allied meetings in Teheran, Yalta and Potsdam, Stalin pledged himself to a policy of continued co-operation. Specifically he agreed to the popular election of governments in the areas overrun by Soviet troops and to a joint administration of occupied Germany. In the Far East he agreed to support Chiang Kai-shek's Chinese government against the Japanese, but only in return for a special position in Manchuria in the post-war settlement. The hard-pressed Chiang Kai-shek had to agree.

As the war came to an end, however, the Soviet government repudiated each of these agreements in turn. In Poland, Hungary, Rumania and Bulgaria regimes were established whose key posts were manned by Communists trained in Moscow. In Germany the joint Four-Power occupation disintegrated into two separate occupations, one in the west by the U.S., Britain and France and another in the east by Russia.

What led Stalin to cast aside all these agreements when his country lay devastated, its population exhausted by the war? Many Western statesmen had believed that at least in the immediate post-war years Stalin would cultivate his alliances with the West as a source of loans, supplies, and aid in rehabilitating his country. In this belief they had put their faith in the Teheran, Yalta and Potsdam agreements. But the war had hardly ended when Stalin ostentatiously turned his back on his allies, again proclaimed his revolutionary goal and decided to go it alone. He strained his relations with the West to the very brink of war at a time when the United States alone had the secret of the atomic bomb, then regarded as the ultimate weapon.

In part Stalin's aggressive drive can be attributed to that fundamental tenet of Marxist belief, world revolution. The fact that every area which the Soviet army took over during the war eventually acquired a Communist regime is ample evidence of this. But Stalin's motives went further. The Russian people's acute awareness of the vulnerability of their frontiers had been newly aroused by the German attack and by Nazi brutality during the war, and it had been enhanced by a deep patriotism caused by their survival from that ordeal. Stalin was therefore impelled to make every effort to secure Russia's frontiers.

TO this end Stalin established a ring of Communist satellite nations from Poland to Bulgaria. His attempt to take over Greece with Moscow-supported guerrilla forces was blocked by anti-Communist forces supported by the United States.

In France and Italy, Stalin tried to exploit post-war economic dislocations so as to bring about popular dissatisfaction as a prelude to the establishment of Communist governments, but the attempt was forestalled by Marshall Plan economic aid. In Iran, Stalin refused to withdraw the Russian troops in temporary wartime occupation, but in 1946 they were forced out by Western diplomatic pressure.

In 1948 pro-Russian groups in Czechoslovakia, once a bastion of democracy in eastern Europe, organized a *coup d'état* which put Communists in undisputed control. That same year Stalin attempted to take over West Berlin by blockading Allied troops in the city. Again he was thwarted, this time by a Western airlift, and eventually he lifted the blockade.

In 1950 he attempted his most daring thrust, an attack into South Korea, using troops from pro-Russian North Korea. But South Korean and United Nations forces succeeded after many months in forcing the attackers back. In Malaya, Burma, Indonesia and the Philippines, Stalin incited Communist rebellions but all were suppressed. He was more successful in Indochina, where Communist-led Vietminh troops assisted by the Chinese Communists were able to impose a partition of the country.

Stalin's greatest success was, of course, in China itself. There, despite his wartime agreements with Chiang Kai-shek, he openly assisted Communist armies to rearm and eventually, despite American aid to Chiang, to drive the Nationalist Chinese off the mainland. He thus gained the entire Chinese mainland for the Communist cause.

Only in one area was Stalin forced to retreat from the position he had held when the war ended. That was Yugoslavia. There the Communist regime led by Marshal Tito, which had established itself during the war with its own army and without significant assistance from Moscow, was at the end of the war his staunchest ally in eastern Europe. But Stalin's attempt to take over control of the Yugoslav army, the secret police and the local Communist apparatus alienated Tito, and Stalin broke with him in 1948.

WHEN Stalin died in 1953 he left an empire larger by far than anything dreamed of by the czars. Though the formal borders of the Soviet Union had not been significantly extended beyond the greatest czarist advances, the country was protected by satellite regimes from the Baltic to the Mediterranean. In the east any danger of attack had been eliminated by the defeat of Japan and by the establishment of a miltant Communist regime in China.

With the death of Stalin, Russian expansionism took on new forms. The grisly old dictator's successors quickly recognized the necessity of avoiding all risks, international and internal, while they established a collective leadership and found a single successor. Instead of pressing forward, they experimented with more flexible methods of control both at home and abroad.

THE results were dramatic, and in some cases tragic. In East Germany in 1953 discontent broke out in demonstrations which were suppressed by Soviet tanks. Unrest in Poland in 1956 led to an upsurge of nationalist feelings against the Stalinist regime—even among Communists—and to the reinstallation of Gomulka, a nationalist Communist whom Stalin had jailed for his independent ways, but the rebellion went no further.

In Hungary the insurgents were less successful. Here a weak liberal Communist regime found itself unable to stem popular resentment against all forms of Russian domination, and a full-scale civil war developed in October and November, 1956, which in the end was put down only by the crushing use of naked Soviet force.

Thereafter, the new Kremlin leaders tried no more experiments with loosening their control over the satellites. At the same time they developed a new form of Soviet expansion called "peaceful coexistence," combining an outwardly friendly attitude with economic competition with the West and economic penetration of the underdeveloped countries of the world. Soviet representatives travelled throughout south-east Asia and the Middle East, offering loans and technical assistance, building steel mills in India and dams in Egypt, and all the while holding the Soviet Union up as a model for ambitious new nations impatient to industrialize their economies. However, as the Kremlin's leaders have themselves in effect said, "Peaceful coexistence is but another road to world Communism."

*One of the last of the doomed Romanov czars, Alexander II, is crowned with gilded pomp in the Kremlin in 1856*

# Panoply of High Power

An arrogant autocracy, trapped with grandeur, has traditionally pulled the vast lands of the Russias together. The czars ruled in the name of God and with the aid of dazzling display—and bureaucratic brutality. The Communists profess an atheistic ideology and awe their subjects with parades of power and police controls. The traditional centralization of power makes possible an expansionist foreign policy, whether under czar or party leader. And today the country's fear of foreign encroachments is played upon by Soviet leaders to induce acceptance of strict internal measures.

THE PINNACLE OF POWER, the Kremlin looms in the golden light of waning day. Its name means fortress, and in the 13th century it had wooden walls. These were later replaced by stone and brick, with watch towers like that in the foreground. Over the centuries the Kremlin acquired many sacred buildings. The Cathedral of the

Annunciation (*far left*) and the Cathedral of the Arch-angel Michael (*left centre*) are now museums. The tallest tower (*centre background*) is named after Ivan the Great. Since Napoleon shelled it in 1812 it has been familiarly known as "Ivan the Slightly Tipsy." On the far right, out-side the Kremlin, is St. Basil's Cathedral, also a museum.

HEIRLOOMS *of a turbulent and splendid past are treasured in the Kremlin in the spirit enunciated by the writer Maxim Gorky: "Citizens, do not touch one stone . . . all this is your history, your pride"*

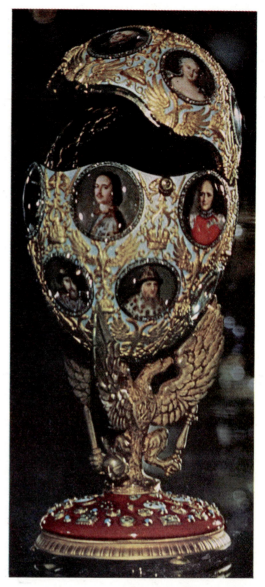

ANNIVERSARY SOUVENIR. The egg above was fashioned in 1913 by the jeweller Fabergé to mark the 300 years of rule by the Romanov dynasty.

CZAR'S BEDROOM (*left*) in the Terem Palace retains its 17th-century elegance. Peter the Great slept in its ornately carved, canopied bed.

CZARS' STUDY, the Golden Room (*opposite*), has an almost barbaric grandeur. Here the czars received their nobles. The window panes are stained mica.

KAZAN CROWN of gold and turquoise, topped by a topaz, was made in 1553 to mark the capture of Kazan on the Volga.

The Great Hall in the Palace of Facets, where huge chandeliers light the vaulted

IVORY THRONE, taken to Moscow by a Byzantine princess who married Ivan III in 1472, was used in Coronations until 1896.

SCEPTRE AND ORB, laden with gems, were made in Constantinople in the 17th century. The orb has a great ruby in its cross.

*ceilings and make the floor shimmer, was once the scene of imperial receptions*

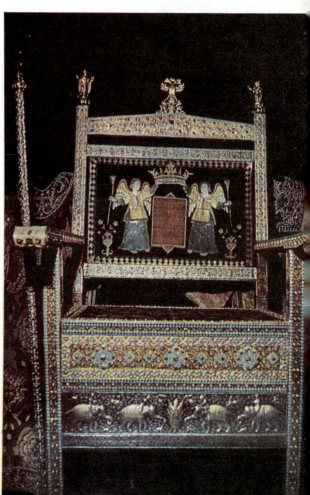

DIAMOND THRONE, also used for Coronations, sparkles with 2,000 diamonds and amethysts. It came from Persia in 1660.

ВПЕРЕД,
К ПОБЕДЕ
КОММУНИЗМА!

# THE MAILED FIST, *brusquely displayed in Moscow,*
*has served to keep the satellite nations under Soviet sway*

POWER DISPLAY is presented by massed Soviet Army soldiers (*opposite*) marching past Lenin's image in Red Square to celebrate the anniversary of the Bolshevik Revolution.

MILITARY MIGHT of Russia strikes in Budapest in 1956 as a Soviet tank roars into the city to crush the Hungarian rebellion. Insurgents had until then been in control.

A SOVIET TRADE FAIR held in Damascus attracts veiled Syrian women. Soviet economic propaganda urges underdeveloped countries to emulate Communist industrialization methods.

*Practising personal diplomacy, Mr Khrushchev beams at*

A SOVIET TECHNICIAN (*foreground*) instructs Indian workers at the Bhilai steel mill being built with Russian aid. Indian technicians are also sent to study in Russia.

SOVIET SALESMANSHIP *in the*
*mid-1950s stressed "peaceful coexistence" while stepping*
*up penetration of underdeveloped countries*

*flower-throwing Indonesian girls on Bali during an extensive Asian tour designed to promote economic and cultural agreements*

*An era ends in 1953 as (from right) Beria, Malenkov, Stalin's son Vasily, Molotov, Bulganin and Kaganovich carry Stalin's coffin*

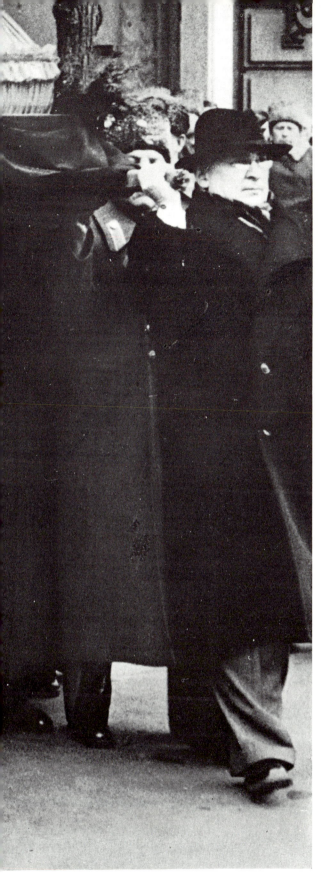

*Khrushchev (behind the coffin) later demoted all of them*

# 3

# Changing Shape of Party Rule

"WHEN *I* use a word," Humpty-Dumpty said in a scornful tone, "it means just what I choose it to mean—neither more nor less." In the Soviet Union, as in Alice's Wonderland, words mean exactly what the Kremlin chooses them to mean, frequently confusing those trying to understand the Communist system.

For example, the Communist party, the repository of ultimate power in the Soviet Union, is not a party at all in the Western sense. It is not "a body of persons forming one side of a contest," since the other side survives, if at all, only in Siberia or in jail. "The place for [opposition parties]," Lenin once said, "is in prison."

Unlike the mass political organizations of the West, the Communist party is a relatively small, highly select band of men and women who rule the entire country with great power. According to its statutes, the party has two distinct functions: to determine high policy for the U.S.S.R., and to supervise the implementation of that policy. Today the party comprises some eight million people, or about four per cent of the population, and its membership largely comprises the elite of Soviet society: government officials, scientists, managers, intellectuals, army and secret police officers. It also includes some outstanding workers and peasants. About a quarter of a million members are full-time paid functionaries, the core of the party's apparatus.

THE organizational principle of the party, as once set forth by Lenin, is "democratic-centralism." This Humpty-Dumpty contradiction in terms (democracy equals rule by the people, but centralism equals rule by the centre) means that authority comes from the top. Lenin in fact stated bluntly that the proletariat, in whose name he ostensibly ruled, could not determine policy. They must be led.

In theory, although seldom in practice, the highest organ of the Communist party is the party Congress, which meets nowadays every two to four years. Apart from approving what the leadership has done in the intervals between sessions, the Congress is supposed to "determine the tactical line of the party on major questions of current policy." In practice no policy question has been openly debated in the Congress since the Soviet regime's early years.

In the interval between meetings of the Congress, the party's Central Committee ostensibly makes policy and directs the Soviet government. This body of about 130 members at present meets two or more times each year. The Central Committee maintains bureaux or sections for supervising every phase of national life. There are sections for the army, for heavy industry, light industry, foreign policy, the arts, propaganda, finances, youth and, most important of all, for personnel. This last group handles the promotion, demotion or transfer of all top party officials, while the other sections control industrial, military and governmental policy and appointments. These sections are directed by members of the Central Secretariat of the party, which meets daily to handle current political and administrative problems and which reports directly to the party leadership.

At the top of the pyramid of Soviet power is the Presidium (previously called the Politburo), which varies in size from six to 25 members and which in theory directs policy between Central Committee sessions. Here, in actual fact, the questions of highest Soviet policy involving hundreds of millions of people are thrashed out and decided. This body in effect represents the "collective leadership" of the Soviet Union.

Since each of these groups is elected by a majority voting in secret, why is it that usually a single man has been able to dominate the entire structure, without any reference to the Russian electorate or even to the party membership?

LENIN himself, confronted before the Revolution by unruly majorities opposed to him, developed a number of subterfuges to gain and maintain control of the party no matter what others wished. Stalin later added a technique which is still a major feature of party life, one which is embodied in the institution of the party secretary. At every level of the party it is the secretary who gives orders. In the Alice-in-Wonderland language of Communist party politics, party secretaries do not take dictation but dictate, and top secretaries generally become absolute dictators.

The power of the secretaries lies in the fact that they control personnel and can determine what questions (and answers) will be dealt with at every party gathering. Although secretaries are ostensibly elected by the body which they serve, they must in all cases be approved by the next higher echelon or—at the top—by the party's Central Committee, which in turn really means by the Central Committee's Secretariat.

Since on each level it is the secretary who in fact controls nominations and hence picks the delegates to higher bodies, a first secretary in the Kremlin who has spotted his adherents in key secretarial posts in the chain of organization can count on them in turn to send equally faithful followers of the first secretary to the various conferences and congresses.

The secretarial power was developed by Stalin when he was appointed to the post of general secretary. Khrushchev originally was only one of several secretaries, but in September of 1953—six months after Stalin's death—he became First Secretary.

While the party makes all policies, it does not administer them. Administration is the function of the Soviet government, which stands parallel to, but separate from, the party apparatus. The government is organized along more conventional lines, beginning with local *soviets* and their executive units and rising through the governments of the republics to the Supreme Soviet, which is the national legislature, and its executive, the Council of Ministers. The chairman of the Council of Ministers is the formal head of the Soviet national administration.

The task of government officials is to carry out the policies enacted by the party. Throughout the Soviet Union the government operates through a series of Ministries and geographical units. The latter consist of republics, autonomous republics and regions (ethnic and territorial sub-divisions of republics) and lesser sub-divisions. These units are occasionally shifted about to correspond with geographic, racial and functional requirements much as any large business organization shifts its component parts to deal with changing problems. In a sense, the formal government provides the arteries through which the lifeblood—the directives of the party—is pumped through the body politic.

DESPITE its seeming cumbersomeness and duality, the system has advantages. Chief among these is that it relieves the policy makers from the routine of administration and leaves them free to ponder important policy matters.

Whenever the Soviet Press announces the dismissal of a top government official or Minister, the probability is not that the official's policies are faulty or that existing policies have changed, but that he has not satisfactorily carried out policies given him to administer. On the other hand, a shift among top party personnel can indicate that a sweeping change of policy has been decreed by the Presidium.

Pointing across the table toward his Foreign Minister, Gromyko, Mr. Khrushchev once remarked to a foreign visitor: "Gromyko is em-

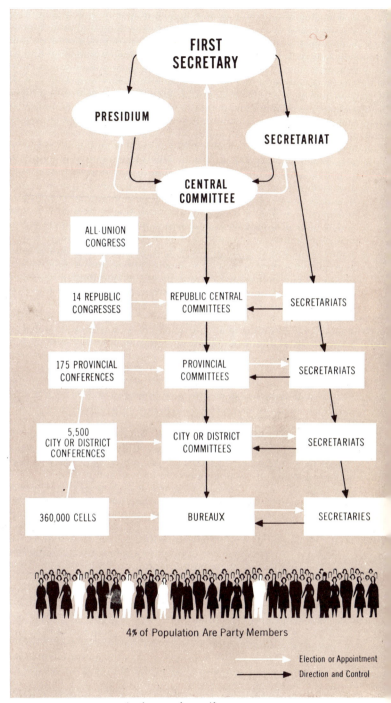

**PARTY ORGANIZATION** is shown above (figures are approximate). All members belong to cells. Each echelon has its own committee or bureau comprising its leadership and its secretariat. At each level the secretary (who rules the secretariat) controls the group which selects him. He therefore can control elections to the next echelon, but he is himself confirmed and controlled by secretaries above him, and ultimately by the First Secretary.

ployed to repeat exactly what we tell him to say. And when he fails to do so we'll dismiss him and find someone who does."

It is not easy to spot shifts in the upper reaches of the party, however, as they are seldom publicly announced. State Ministers, as the front-men of the regime, are often in the public eye, and their appointments and dismissals are reported in the daily Press. But the real decision makers, hidden behind the veil of party secrecy, can convene in a corner of the Kremlin, make a decision which may affect the future of the entire world, and disperse again without the most perceptive foreigner having suspected that they have even met. Only on those occasions when the collective leadership shows itself in public—on top of Lenin's tomb in Red Square or on the platform at an important party gathering—does the average Russian get an inkling of each member's relative standing in the hierarchy.

TOGETHER with these advantages, the system of dual authority also has its drawbacks. On every level of government from the Council of Ministers to the lowest factory board, the party representative upholds first and foremost the political point of view for which he has been trained. His counterpart, on the other hand— the Minister, the manager, the engineer or the scientist—is primarily concerned with technical operations. The supremacy of the party has in the past been clear enough to supress any resentments the technical class may feel toward political interference. But there always remains the possibility of friction between them.

The structure of Soviet power at any given moment is a reflection of problems facing the party at the time. Before Lenin could claim undisputed party control he found it necessary to improvise, reinterpret or slyly contravene the rules he and his comrades had previously agreed to. Stalin so dominated the party and manipulated its structure that in the end he all but destroyed it as an instrument of policy.

In his devious campaign to supplant Trotsky as Lenin's successor, Stalin took care to develop the role of the party secretaries. At one point in the

contest the party rank and file returned to regional conferences delegates of whom 36 per cent sided with Trotsky. But efficient nomination of Stalinist candidates by the regional secretaries reduced the pro-Trotsky delegates to a mere 18 per cent at the next level. Trotsky with some justice deduced that at the primary level he had had a large majority, but that already at the regional level this majority had been reduced severely to the 36 per cent, and by the time it reached the top echelon it had been whittled down to an insignificant minority.

These ruses sufficed Stalin during the 1920s. But when he was faced in the 1930s with party opposition to the harsh measures he had instituted during his industrialization and collectivization drives (*see Chapters 4 and 5*), he needed more ruthless methods of repression to maintain discipline. As a consequence he resorted to police terror on a major scale.

The result was one of the most brutal periods of Russian history. Thousands of devoted Old Bolsheviks were arrested, forced to make humiliating and often absurd confessions and, in a series of public trials, persuaded to grovel before the sadistic Georgian. Thousands of Soviet Army officers were cashiered and either shot or exiled to Siberia. (When the second World War came, Stalin recalled several officers, including Marshal Rokossovsky, and entrusted them with high commands.) Hundreds of thousands of lesser citizens were arrested and either liquidated or exiled and sentenced to forced labour without any recourse to trial.

WHILE he purged and murdered, Stalin also raised an impenetrable curtain between his subjects and foreigners. He did so partly to prevent the Russian people from making unfavourable comparisons between his regime and life abroad, and partly because of his pathological fear of foreign agents. Any Soviet citizen found conversing with a foreigner was automatically suspect, and when an innocent Russian saw a foreign friend approaching down the street he generally darted panic-stricken into an alley.

One of the purge's by-products was that for the

rest of Stalin's lifetime the party was virtually eliminated as a policy-making authority. An absolute dictator with a phenomenal grasp of detail, Stalin was able to rule without its services, using such channels as expedience required. In fact his secret police, best known by their initials GPU and later MVD, were frequently made responsible for carrying out his orders and even for managing entire industrial enterprises.

THE outbreak of the second World War brought some relief from terror, but no relaxation of Stalin's personal grip. Factory directors in remote areas could expect frequently to hear the telephone ring in the middle of the night and to hear the gruff, threatening tones of the dictator himself, who demanded to know why a plan had not been fulfilled, or why a new weapon or piece of equipment was not functioning properly.

Nor did the end of the war and the victory bring any respite. Exhausted by four years of superhuman effort and worn down by the constant strain of Stalin's incessant threatening and prodding, the people had looked forward eagerly to some easing of controls and to greater incentives. But Stalin never eased up. Instead he drove the Russian people harder than ever to rebuild their cities and rehabilitate their factories. Peasants who during the war had enjoyed little supervision were gathered together again into the hated collective system.

Late in 1952 Stalin announced the discovery of a plot against leading army officers and the arrest of a group of prominent doctors. The men around him feared another purge. But the crisis was short-lived. On a cold day in March 1953, the head of Stalin's bodyguard telephoned to the leading party lieutenants, Molotov, Malenkov, Khrushchev and the police chief Beria, to announce that the master had had a stroke.

The four men hurried dutifully to Stalin's bedside, but he was paralyzed and unconscious. Beria, who had been Stalin's police chief since 1938, assumed his master was about to die and started to revile him. Suddenly Stalin stirred and raised an arm. Beria, terrified that he would revive, fell to his knees by the bedside grovelling before the sick man, slobbering and kissing his hands. Only then Stalin died.

"I wept," Khrushchev later told a foreign visitor. "Like Peter he fought barbarism with barbarism. But he was a great man."

Dazed and not a little terrified at the prospect of having to rule the downtrodden masses Stalin left behind, his followers appealed to the party and the people not to panic. At once they faced the problem for which their system had no solution: how to select a successor?

THE temporary recourse they hit upon was "collective leadership," which at first consisted of Malenkov, Molotov, Beria and Khrushchev. Malenkov was the first among "equals." But they also began to relax the pressures under which their subjects had been suffering. Within four months Beria was arrested and later he was shot. Then the leadership pledged themselves not to liquidate one another any more. The police were restricted and brought under control of the entire Presidium so that no one man could again wield Stalin's terror, and in a famous 1956 speech Khrushchev denounced the former dictator's despotism. Plans were begun to increase housing and to produce more consumer goods.

While his colleagues began to revive the sagging party structure, Malenkov turned to the government apparatus as the means by which to rule. But Khrushchev, who took over the party organization as First Secretary, had other ideas both of policy and of power. Playing much the same game as Stalin, Khrushchev stuffed the party apparatus with men loyal to him and gradually elbowed his colleagues out of their positions of power.

Resentful of his methods and fearful that another Stalin was about to arise, his rivals in the Presidium turned on him in 1957 and demanded his resignation. Faced by a seven-to-four majority against him, Khrushchev took a fateful step. Invoking the long-ignored party statutes, he appealed to the Central Committee, where he felt confident he could muster a majority. He also appealed to the army and won its support.

## The Changing Shape of Party Rule

The stratagem worked. Malenkov and Molotov were expelled from the Central Committee —and thus from the Presidium—and sent away from Moscow to minor posts. But the price Khrushchev paid was enormous. In an unprecedented move he had gone outside the ruling clique represented by the Presidium and acknowledged the right of the larger, less-easily-dominated Central Committee to choose the ruler of the party. What would happen the next time a leader needed to be chosen?

ANOTHER significant development now under way was that the composition of the party membership was undergoing a change. When Stalin liquidated the "Old Guard" during his struggle with Trotsky and in the later purges, the positions of leadership were taken by young men who had not sacrificed their early years to the hardships of underground life.

Many of the Central Committee members who supported Khrushchev had spent their mature lives under Soviet rule. Their faith in Marx was strong but it had not been case-hardened in the pre-revolutionary struggle. More systematically educated, they tended to have a better grasp of the technical aspects of a modern economy and perhaps a less dogmatic approach to the "scientific laws" of Marxism. They may therefore be less susceptible to party discipline and less blindly loyal to Communist dogma.

Even further removed from Lenin's time are the young party recruits of today. The normal starting point for the Communist leaders of tomorrow is the Komsomol or Young Communist League. Here those with political ambitions are trained and tested in their teens. At least in the early years the recruit is expected to devote most if not all of his free time to party work, organizing and attending meetings, delivering speeches to workers' gatherings and doing odd jobs for the local party headquarters.

Nowadays, with more opportunities available for leisure, by no means all Soviet youths relish the burdens of party membership. Furthermore, many of them recall the high death rate among party members during Stalin's regime and prefer to stand aside from political life, devoting themselves to more tranquil careers as engineers, doctors or scientists.

Finally, in the puritanical society of Russia today the party member is expected to be the most puritanical of all. While others may occasionally get drunk, skip a day's work or even go to church, the party member is required to set an example of Spartan morality. If he fails to do so he can expect to lose his party card.

For these reasons the successful young party member today is generally a dedicated, mentally agile careerist with considerable administrative experience. If he has demonstrated these qualities, the chances are that when he has finished his regular education he will be sent to a special school to study party doctrine and the techniques of Communist government. Later he will be used for party work and assigned as a party secretary to some remote area. Frequent transfers are the rule, and before he finally reaches national prominence he will have served in a dozen towns and cities throughout the country.

By the time he has become a member of the Central Committee or a candidate for the Presidium, the keen young Communist party member has gone through a rigorous training and several party schools, which will have made him a tough, efficient and devoted official, a disciplined political soldier and a selfless servant of his cause.

THE re-emergence of the party, the potential upgrading of the Central Committee and the change in party membership do not signify any great democratization of the Soviet government or the elimination of one-man rule. They have merely demonstrated that the structure of power in the Soviet Union is not immutable. Indeed, it never seems to stop changing.

With new men facing the new problems of a society emerging from primitive want, further changes are inevitable—but how far, how fast and in what direction the new men will move are questions even they cannot answer.

*The two most powerful forces in the development of the party, Lenin and Stalin, meet outside Moscow in 1922*

# The Party's Leaders and Ranks

Lenin organized and developed the Communist party as a tightly disciplined body dedicated to the principle of revolution. Orders came from the top but the leadership was somewhat responsive to new ideas initiated from below, provided these did not disturb the centralization of power. Stalin remade the party into his own instrument, then later virtually ignored it as he ruled through personal autocracy. Khrushchev, though originally a disciple of Stalin, reverted to the Lenin concept of "party democracy" and revivified the party as a means of governing.

47

APPLYING FOR MEMBERSHIP in a Rostov party cell, forge press operator Mikhail Dedushko tells local officers of the party about his qualifications and his experience.

HEARING THE MESSAGE (below) workers in Leningrad gather to hear a party member explain what happened at a recent meeting of the Central Committee in Moscow.

AT A LOCAL LEVEL *the party operates through cells organized at members' places of employment. Party members watch over the operation of factories and shops to make sure the Kremlin's policies and plans are carried out*

WATCHING A WORKER. An engineer in a Rostov machinery works who is also a member of the factory's party committee checks for the party on an employee's efficiency.

HOW A LEADER RISES can be
seen by comparing pictures
of party chiefs. Reviewing a
1937 parade, Stalin (*centre*)
was flanked on the left by
Dimitrov (head of the Comi-
tern) and Molotov (Premier).
But a new personality was
Khrushchev (*second from left*)
who a year later would be
elected to the Politburo.

SOVIET LEADERS *make a habit of displaying themselves on ceremonial occasions, thereby informing Russia and the outside world of the relative power positions of individuals*

IN 1953, with Stalin gone, the party was run by a "collective leadership." Top man that November presumably was Malenkov (*10th from left*), but he shared prominence with Molotov, Khrushchev and L. Kaganovich (*left to right beside him*).

IN 1960 Khrushchev is unmistakably in charge. Appearing at a rally after a trip abroad, the First Secretary leads the applause in the centre. Most of his 1953 rivals have gone, and he appears with new men, one of whom may some day take his position.

In the murky interior of the Kharkov Tractor Factory two women tend big metalworking machines. Constructed early in Stalin's

*industrialization drive, this factory may be modernized soon*

# 4

# A Growing State-Run Economy

FROM all outward appearances an industrial factory in Communist Russia differs little from its capitalist counterpart. There is not much, for example, to distinguish the ZIL Car Factory on the outskirts of Moscow from a 25-year-old car factory in Coventry.

The ZIL factory, whose initials commemorate a former director, consists of a sprawling conglomeration of sooty brick buildings, situated behind a high brick wall and containing machine shops, furnaces and assembly lines. Inside the vast gloomy halls the deafening roar of machinery echoes against the walls. Thousands of lamps supplement the sunlight struggling through the dirty skylights. Drills, lathes and giant presses are tended by young men and women in dirty overalls. Cranes, conveyors and assembly belts creep relentlessly along their tracks.

Perhaps the only distinguishing feature of the Soviet factory is the plethora of banners on the walls calling for greater output and naming those prize workers who have over-fulfilled their quotas. These banners bespeak an economic system which is fundamentally different from those in the West.

Most visitors to the U.S.S.R. in recent years have come back with astonishing reports of the rapid growth of the Soviet economy. Fifty years ago, in the last years of peace under the czars, Russia's economy ranked fifth in the world. Today the Soviet Union boasts an industrial empire second only to that of the United States and claims its economy is growing so fast that it will overtake and surpass the U.S. in another decade, thereby proving the superiority of Communism over capitalism.

It is difficult to judge the accuracy of these claims. The traditional Russian passions for secrecy and for making a good show have been brought to a new intensity by the Communists, rendering Soviet statistics peculiarly vulnerable to the remark quoted by Mark Twain that there are lies, damn lies and statistics. Stalin, as his successors have since confessed, often deliberately falsified statistics. Sometimes when the true figures are past doctoring, as in the case of family incomes, they are simply suppressed.

BUT if a precise accounting is impossible, an outsider can at least find out how the Soviet system works by examining an establishment such as the ZIL factory. This is neither the best nor the worst in the Soviet Union. The State Ball Bearing Factory No. 1 in Moscow, for instance, is much better equipped with modern automatic machinery than the ZIL factory. In other Soviet factories working conditions are much worse. The visitor to the Stalingrad Tractor Factory who comes on a rainy day is likely to see water dripping through the leaky skylights onto the kerchiefed heads of the young girls tending the giant presses. Safety precautions in many Soviet factories are woefully inadequate by Western standards.

The ZIL factory has recreational facilities for its workers far more extensive than those of even the most modern European factories. These include restaurants, playing fields, gymnasiums and a 2,500-seat theatre housed in a building with the pretentious title of Palace of Culture. ZIL has its own soccer team, a leading team which plays in the Soviet A League. The team's fans are no less vociferous than Londoners cheering Tottenham Hotspur. In July 1958 the star of the team and the leading Soviet centre-forward, Eduard Streltsov, was so lavished with rewards and honours that it went to his head and after a series of debauched brawls he wound up with a 12-year jail sentence. When this occurred Streltsov was mourned by the entire ZIL factory, including its director, Alexei Krylov, who boasts that he seldom misses a game.

DIRECTOR Krylov himself is scarcely distinguishable from a factory manager in Britain. Stout but vigorous, he has a jaunty, hail-fellow approach to his subordinates as well as to strangers. Ordinarily he wears a well-tailored double-breasted blue suit.

The 40,000 men and women who work for Krylov look much like workers in any factory abroad or in the Soviet Union. But they doubtless consider themselves a cut above their fellow workers in some of the new industrial areas of Siberia or Kazakhstan, who live in poorly-heated wooden barracks, eat in dirty canteens, and slosh to work through miles of knee-deep mud.

The skilled workers in the ZIL Car Factory are paid top wages and can shop in Moscow in the best-stocked stores in the entire Communist empire. Many of them live scarcely half a mile from their work in factory-subsidized flats. While their living standards are far inferior to those of a skilled car-worker in Coventry, they are incomparably better off than many of their compatriots in the provinces.

In every Soviet industry there are half a dozen or more wage classifications. Each worker is classified according to the degree of skill his job requires. Because most of the ZIL jobs have a high classification, Krylov can assure his workers top treatment. But as the system is based both on piece rates and on time, wages vary within any classification according to the amount a person produces as well as the length of time he works.

Wages also vary geographically, and workers

living in rural areas where the cost of living is lower generally receive lower pay. Those in very remote areas like the construction site at Bratsk in Siberia are often paid double wages in the form of "hardship" premiums.

The factory's products resemble in design, though not in quality, their European and American counterparts, for the Russians have for years slavishly copied Western car designs. The ZIL works each year turns out 120,000 vehicles including passenger cars, buses and trucks. It also makes half a million bicycles and a hundred thousand electric refrigerators. Director Krylov is the first to admit that this diversity is inefficient, and plans are now underway to build only trucks and that dream of the Soviet housewife—electric refrigerators.

But as Director Krylov can testify, the economic system on which the ZIL plant operates differs radically from that of a Western factory in three fundamental respects. First, the enterprise is State-owned. Second, it is operated according to a centrally-directed plan. Third, at least until now it has produced primarily not for the consumer but for heavy industries. Thus ZIL turns out a far greater number of trucks than passenger cars.

OWNING and controlling not only the means of production but almost all retail outlets as well, the Soviet government has eliminated almost every vestige of private enterprise, and has turned its back on the principle of supply and demand which in other economies determines what is to be produced and what the ultimate price will be. For these conventional objects and controls the Kremlin has substituted a centrally-directed, planned economy in which the national interest as determined by the Kremlin replaces the private incentives of the producer and ignores the private preference of the consumer.

With no competition to meet, the ZIL factory has its prices set as the government sees fit. When ZIL sells to another State enterprise the price is usually fixed at about five per cent above costs. But when it sells to individuals, which it does not do directly but through a State-owned agency, the price is usually based on considerations of political expediency.

For example, ZIL produces a small passenger car that sells to the public for £1,600. It also makes a large bus, obviously much more costly to produce, that sells to the government transport organizations for only £1,000. The passenger car's price has been set at about double its actual cost to discourage public demand for a commodity that is made only in small quantities.

THE number of units of each car or any other product turned out is determined in Soviet Russia not by demand but by "the plan." There are two kinds of plans: long-range five- or seven-year plans, and short-term yearly and quarterly plans. The short-term plans are what govern a factory like ZIL, and ZIL's plans have to be worked out each year by Krylov and his staff.

Krylov bases his calculations each year on the number of vehicles and other items he has been called upon to produce by GOSPLAN, the Soviet State Planning Committee. With his chief planners and engineers, he works out a detailed list of all the materials he will need to fulfil his quota. He sends this tentative plan to his regional economic council (the U.S.S.R. is divided into about a hundred economic regions), which consolidates it with plans of other factories in the region and sends it on to GOSPLAN. GOSPLAN balances ZIL's requirements against the planned production of each item throughout the Soviet Union and makes sure all the basic materials Krylov needs will be available. GOSPLAN also allots major capital investment funds to new projects, or to existing plants that need expansion.

While the short-term plans constitute actual operating schedules, long-term ones are worked out in more general terms and are chiefly propaganda devices to spur production through appeals to the workers' patriotism. Long-range planning began in 1929 and since then there have been six Five-Year Plans and one Seven-Year Plan (the latter began in 1959).

After a plan has been approved, party organizers in a factory like ZIL distribute a copy of it to every office and shop and carefully explain and discuss it. Each worker is told precisely what is expected of him and is shown how his output fits into the factory's—and the nation's—production quota. With the plans, particularly the short-term ones, being talked up in a psychological atmosphere, workers are effectively stimulated to support the plan's goals—and to avoid the social stigma that comes from falling short.

Ever since planning was first introduced in Russia, heavy industry has been given an absolute priority over industries that produce consumer goods. The reason for this was Stalin's determination to achieve rapid industrialization, coupled with his impatience to create a sound basis for an arms industry with which to defend "the citadel of Communism."

The effect of the heavy industry priority is that in allocating supplies of all basic commodities from iron ore to labour, GOSPLAN gives first choice of all scarce items to industries producing machines for production. Only what is left over is assigned to the manufacture of consumer goods. More important, in the allocation of investment capital, heavy industry has always been given much the largest share.

HOW has the Communist planned economy worked in comparison with capitalism? Soviet economists point out that the United States took about sixty years, from 1850 to 1910, to create a mature industrial economy, whereas by their reckoning they have accomplished the same task in half the time, beginning in 1929 and ending up in the early 1950s.

Western economists, however, suggest that Russian industrialization actually began at the end of the 19th century, and that by the first World War the country had a substantial production of such basic goods as coal, steel and oil. Though most of the factories lay idle during the Revolution and the subsequent civil war, the machinery, manpower and technical experience were none the less at hand when the Bolsheviks re-started the country's march toward industrialization. Therefore, say these economists, the rate of Russian industrialization has been more or less the same as that of all other countries undergoing a similar development—except that the cost in lives and hardships to the Russian population has

been incomparably greater than it has been in any non-Communist country. This was due largely to the methods chosen by the Bolsheviks after they took power in 1917.

WHILE Karl Marx laid down many specific rules for setting up a Communist State politically, he did not give his followers any advice on how to organize a Socialist economy. As Lenin himself said during the Revolution: "We have knowledge of Socialism, but as for knowledge of . . . the organization and distribution of commodities—that we have not. This the old Bolshevik leaders did not teach us. . . ."

Improvising as he went along, Lenin first invited the old factory managers to stay on as employees of the State. But the response was unenthusiastic. This left the factories in the hands of untrained party members. With the onset of the civil war production rapidly declined, consumer goods all but disappeared and the currency became almost worthless.

Nevertheless, with fanatical faith in Marx, Lenin proclaimed that from the start Soviet industry would be run on the old Marxist principle: "From each according to his ability; to each according to his needs." This attempt to use Marxist theories to meet recurring crises was called "War Communism." Since the population's most pressing need was for food which the peasantry alone produced, Lenin ordered the peasants to deliver all surplus supplies to requisitioning groups from the cities, and to accept almost worthless money in payment. Many peasants refused, the city markets lay empty and famine spread. The toll in lives reached staggering figures.

By 1921, surrounded by evidence of the complete breakdown of War Communism, Lenin finally ordered a general retreat and introduced his "New Economic Policy," whereby at least small manufacturing and retailing enterprises were returned to private hands, and peasants were permitted to exchange their grain for manufactured goods. Conditions improved quickly and the peasants, once again able to buy the goods they needed, began selling their food to the cities. The few large factories still in government hands were put back into production, though only on a small scale. In 1924—the year that Lenin died—the Moscow Car Repair factory, which is now the ZIL works, began turning out cars; but only ten were produced that year.

Obviously at that rate the industrialization of the country, which Lenin's successor Stalin considered essential for Communist survival, would be slow indeed. Stalin also knew, however, that the sweeping programme he envisaged would require a ruthless dictatorship. Not until 1927 had he established himself firmly enough in power to begin plans for his programme.

Like the head of any nation attempting to build a modern industrial State, Stalin faced tremendous problems. He had to accumulate capital to construct the factories he needed. He had to develop a reservoir of technological skills. He had to establish a system for allocating raw materials and he had to obtain workers for the new factories.

TO raise capital for expansion, Stalin had two alternatives: he could get money abroad, or he could raise it at home. Because foreign investors were reluctant to risk capital in the Communist system, Stalin was forced to choose the second course. This meant that he had to drive workers under fearful conditions into the factories and mines. He prescribed heavy fines for tardiness and jail sentences for absenteeism. Periodically he raised the work quotas and lowered the pay scale.

Stalin's methods caused much revulsion and disaffection not only among the workers themselves but among his colleagues in the party hierarchy, and this was probably the chief justification for the police terror which he instituted in the early 1930s. Nevertheless, by selling consumer goods at enormous profits and by levying a heavy compulsory delivery on crops, he did manage to gain control of the resources needed to accumulate capital.

Even today profits from consumer goods—obtained by what are in effect sales taxes—provide the bulk of Soviet investment funds. For example, when a £5 a week caretaker in Leningrad needs four yards of cloth for a new work smock she may

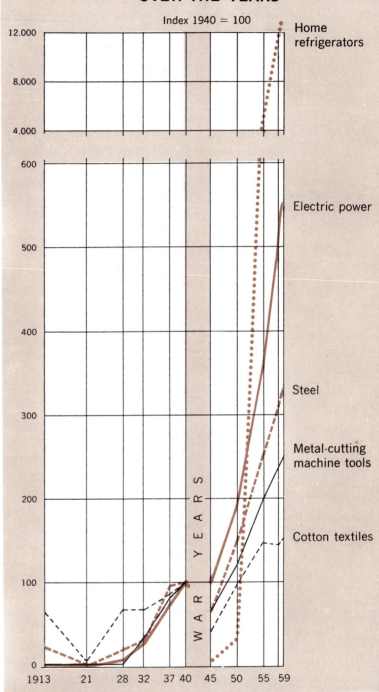

**SOVIET INDUSTRIAL PRODUCTION OVER THE YEARS**

Index 1940 = 100

Home refrigerators
Electric power
Steel
Metal-cutting machine tools
Cotton textiles

WAR YEARS

12,000  8,000  4,000  600  500  400  300  200  100  0

1913  21  28  32  37  40  45  50  55  59

PRODUCTION GROWTH of key Soviet industries is shown above (1940 output equals 100). Steel-making for example went from its lowest point in 1921 and through a sharp climb in the 1930s to reach its 1940 figure. Since the war it has tripled.

find that the cheapest cloth she can get is plain, unbleached white cotton selling for six shillings a yard. She does not know it, for cost figures are kept secret, but the cotton probably cost the government only two shillings a yard to produce. The rest goes to the State for investment uses.

In building a technological base, Stalin was able to take advantage of the technical advances already achieved by more developed countries of the West. In the late 1920s and early 1930s hundreds of engineers from Europe and America went to Russia, bringing with them the latest industrial techniques of the West. In 1932 an American built Russia's first big modern hydro-electric plant, on the Dnieper. Engineers from a number of American car companies were employed to teach the Soviet car industry how to use modern mass production techniques.

Years later, during and immediately after the second World War, the United States sent large quantities of machine tools and equipment to strengthen Russia's war industries.

One of the characteristics of Stalin's industrialization drive was the assignment of priorities not only to sectors of the economy but to individual projects, not just in the field of industry but in education, science and technology. When Stalin launched his first Five-Year Plan, Russia was still dependent on foreign sources for many essential raw materials. Suspecting that the country contained undiscovered resources of its own, Stalin placed a high priority on the education of mineralogists and the development of prospecting methods. Within a decade teams of trained geologists were travelling the country and finding deposits of many of the resources Soviet industry needed.

When Stalin at the end of the second World War found himself confronted with an American monopoly of atomic weapons, he lost no time in giving the highest priority to nuclear research, and a special Ministry was organized to provide Soviet scientists with laboratories and equipment. Meanwhile in the schools and universities special premiums and privileges were offered to promising students if they devoted themselves to nuclear physics and related fields.

Similarly Stalin and his successors gave top priority to space research and rocketry, thereby producing the spectacular lead the Soviet Union has taken in this field. Such achievements, however, must be at the expense of consumer goods production. The day the Soviet rocket photographed the far side of the moon, a foreigner scoured Moscow in vain searching for a standard flashlight battery, and was told, "They are not made in the Soviet Union."

While Russia today has many highly-qualified and inventive technologists, Soviet directors and managers are often reluctant to make the most of new techniques, new designs or new inventions. Once a Soviet director has elaborated plans for the production of a commodity and has laboriously won approval for his production programme, he does not relish the appearance of something new that might entail scrapping his entire programme and working out a new one.

THE key to Stalin's economic administration —and particularly to his way of allocating raw materials—was centralization. Moscow told every factory director where and in what quantities to get the supplies he needed. If his requirements changed he had to correspond through half a dozen layers of administration to the Ministry within whose jurisdiction he came. The order would travel through layers of bureaucracy to the plant where the item was produced. The entire process often took months.

In the relatively primitive economy of the first Five-Year Plans the task of operating such a system was costly but tolerable. But as Russia's industrial plant expanded and as the variety and complexity of commodities increased, the difficulty of directing the economy from one central point grew in geometric progression.

By the time Stalin died in 1953 the whole unwieldy structure was losing its momentum under the weight of the central bureaucracy. In 1957 Khrushchev finally decided that some degree of economic decentralization was necessary. The maze of centralized Ministries was dismantled and in its place the regional councils were set up —manned mostly by officials of the former

Ministries, who reluctantly moved from Moscow into the provinces.

WITHIN the confines of national planning, the chairmen of these councils have been given considerable power over all economic activities in their respective regions. In turn they have been instructed to delegate many of their powers to the factory directors and business managers under them. Today the directors have the right to do business directly with other enterprises inside their region.

"In the old days a factory in the Urals, 850 miles away, was designated to supply me with paint," Director Krylov once explained. "Under the new arrangement I have found a factory nearly next door which can furnish me with exactly the same type of paint."

The present system has undoubtedly reduced the degree of direct control the Kremlin can exercise on the economy through the Ministries. But the decentralization programme also included a strengthening both of the Communist party apparatus and of GOSPLAN. Both maintain a network of checkers and inspectors in every factory and enterprise in the U.S.S.R.

Scarcities still exist under the decentralization programme. One way in which Russian businessmen try to solve the problem is through the use of "expediters." A mishap in a Ural copper plant, for example, may leave the director of a Leningrad electrical works without enough copper wire to produce the number of armatures required by his yearly plan. Since the plan provides for little slack and few reserves, the director calls in his expediter, whose business it is to have friends among the director's main suppliers. In this case the expediter knows the director of the copper plant, who tells him that his production could be increased if he could obtain a certain mining machine from the Uralmash Plant in Sverdlovsk. The expediter goes to Sverdlovsk, where he finds that the director, another old friend, is short of electrical motors. The problem is solved. Leningrad ships the needed motor to Sverdlovsk, the mining equipment goes to the copper plant and the wire is quickly on its way to Leningrad. From each of the directors the expediter collects his fee.

Considered unproductive middlemen whose activities sometimes interfere with the operation of plans, expediters are frowned upon by the Kremlin, which has decreed that any director caught employing one will have the amount of the expediter's fee docked from his salary. "The fees are so high," a Leningrad factory director complained recently, "that I simply can't afford to get caught more than once a year."

AMONG the biggest problems which faced Stalin was that of obtaining skilled labour. As factories mushroomed in the 1930s, hundreds of thousands of peasants were recruited from the villages to man the new machines. As they were poorly educated and inexperienced, their productivity was well below that of Western workers. Large numbers of women were recruited and often given the heaviest and most distasteful forms of labour. In fact to this day Soviet women enjoy a near-monopoly in the field of road-building and street-cleaning.

To increase the output of this untrained labour force, Stalin and his subordinates encouraged individual workers to overfulfill their work quotas, which in some instances they did by several hundred per cent. These "Stakhanovites"—so-called after Alexei Stakhanov, the first such shock-worker—set prodigious production records.

A drop in the Russian birthrate during the war years added to the scarcity of labour in the late 1950s just when Stalin's successors were decreeing the greatest expansion of production. Khrushchev ordered that the goals of the plan were to be achieved not by a costly expansion of the labour force but through increased productivity on the part of the existing force, using more efficient tools and better working methods.

The result of these directives has been to put heavy pressure on factory directors to fulfill greatly increased production quotas with the same amount of labour force and thus greatly to increase the efficiency of their factories. But it has also brought about severe competition for skilled labour. Director Krylov states that the only way he can get enough skilled labourers is to promise them better conditions than do his fellow directors. He pays top wages and is building workers' housing not far from the factory.

IN launching the Seven-Year Plan in 1959, the Soviet government stated that "By 1968–70 the U.S.S.R. will also have surpassed the U.S.A. in per capita output of industrial goods."

Soviet statisticians have proved, at least to their own satisfaction, that the continued rise of Soviet industrial production at a greater rate than that of the United States will permit them to close within a decade the gap existing between the two countries. There can be no doubt that in recent years the Soviet economy has made astounding strides.

Western economists are sceptical, however, of these forecasts and point out that rapid growth is a feature of every economy in the early stages of development, and that as Soviet production approaches that of other mature countries it too will tend to level off.

To the Western resident in Russia, confronted by shortages of many goods and a complete lack of others, the Kremlin's boast sounds oddly reminiscent of the slogan with which Stalin ushered in the notorious era of purge and terror in the mid-1930s: "Life is better, comrades, life is gayer."

*A sign of Soviet progress, a giant turbine rotor is exhibited in Moscow. The rotor was made for a Volga power station*

# Priority: Capital Goods

Massive machinery, as shown at a public fair (*above*), is impressive evidence of a Soviet economic system that emphasizes capital goods and minimizes personal consumption. The Kremlin's concentration on heavy industry is designed to support the country's large military programme and to create a firm base for further economic growth. Western economists say that while Russia's economy has made great strides in the past thirty years, its industrial expansion has been artificial and distorted, tending to bring about a basic imbalance in the country's economic life.

WATERWAYS *like the broad Volga River, while continuing to serve as means of transport, provide valuable sources of much-needed electrical energy, which is now being harnessed*

BIG POWER STATION at Kuibyshev (*right*), shown at its dedication in 1958 —three years late.

WOOD EN ROUTE goes down-river (*left*), much as it has done for centuries, in rafts half a mile long. The crews and their folk live in huts on board.

CRANE IN TRANSIT, a symbol of the industrial effort, waits in the night to pass the lighted locks which are a part of Kuibyshev's power system.

SAMARKAND SILK SPINNER, an Uzbek woman, operates modern silk-milling machinery in the legendary Soviet Central Asian city that was the capital of Tamerlane's 14th-century Mongolian Empire. The factory is part of the industrial development of Central Asia. In addition to producing silk, Samarkand is a centre of cotton ginning.

WOMEN AT WORK *perform a wide range of jobs in Russia, building roads, cleaning streets—but also working on a completely equal basis with men in such highly-paid and specialized fields as medicine and engineering*

SURVEYOR works on plans for a dam to be built in Alma-Ata, capital of Kazakhstan. The dam will help prevent recurring floods which periodically inundate the city streets.

STREET WORKER in Moscow uses a heavy pneumatic drill alongside a male companion. The State encourages women to work so as to help alleviate the chronic labour shortage.

TWO PRODUCTS, side by side, are turned
out at the ZIL factory in Moscow, bicycles
in the foreground, cars in the background.

# CONSUMER GOODS,

*long denied the Russian*
*people in quantity, are*
*now being produced to a*
*greater degree, but*
*there are still many*
*shortages everywhere*

FREE ENTERPRISE exists on a small
scale to make up for some shortages.
The boys in Moscow above are selling coat hangers that were probably
made nearby in a small handicraft
shop controlled by the government.

RUSSIAN SPECIALITY, caviar, is packed by girls in a fish factory in Astrakhan on the Caspian Sea.

TECHNOLOGY, *given a high priority by Stalin, has been justified in past accomplishments in nuclear and space research and holds promise of future advances*

CATALYST VATS are supervised by a technician in the Novo-Baku Oil Refinery in Baku. The petroleum industry has flourished in Russia since before the Revolution.

HIGH–VOLTAGE STUDY is being carried out at the Institute of Electrical Engineering, Leningrad, where technicians are investigating new ways of transmitting power.

HUGE COMPUTER, the largest and most elaborate in the U.S.S.R., is operated by two specially trained men at the Computing Centre of the Academy of Sciences, Moscow.

*Typical of the many millions of acres of potentially productive land in the Soviet Union not being used to full advantage*

# Trial and Error on the Farm

5

*is this rolling expanse of open country in southern Russia, on which Kabardinian herdsmen feed calves for breeding*

No problem has beset the rulers of Russia more in recent centuries than that of assuring a steady flow of food for the country's relentlessly expanding population. Although it has more land than any other country in the world, Russia has only recently been able to feed itself adequately.

From the days of serfdom till the downfall of the czars, successive governments tried a variety of remedies and reforms, but always without success. Equally unsuccessfully, the Russians have continued the search for a solution by herding almost the entire rural population into a nation-wide system of collective farms.

Though collective farms are the hallmark of Russian agriculture today, they are rarely seen by outsiders. Such secretiveness is no new phenomenon, however. When Catherine the Great wanted to visit her peasant villages, her chief adviser, Grigory Potemkin, hastily built temporary facades of fake villages to hide the realities of the poverty-stricken countryside. When foreigners today ask to see the collectives they are shown—with equally ill-feigned guile—model communities of brand-new barns and machine shops, neat cottages, co-operative stores and even hospitals and maternity wards. Their guides glibly call these "average farms." The really average collectives are hidden from prying eyes for fear that they might reveal all too clearly the Communists' failure to find a satisfactory solution to the peasant problem.

TO all appearances a real Soviet collective farm is not a farm at all but a straggling village built on either side of a wide street. The width of the street is no accident. Meandering back and forth along it like the channel of a river are the tracks of carts, tractors and the occasional cars of party and government officials, which during a spring thaw dig deep ruts in the mud. When the ruts become too deep and muddy, the tracks move to the other side of the street until that side too becomes impassable. Meanwhile the old ruts dry out.

The huts themselves vary from the black log structures of Siberia to the flat-roofed adobe huts of Central Asia and the stone cottages of Georgia. In European Russia the log houses turn grey with age. At first glance every village looks exactly like the last one, but if you look closely you will find that each has its special type of hut, distinguished by the way the dormer windows are cut into the roof, the size of the porch (if any) and the position and size of the enclosed passage at the side.

Along the street are open wells, sometimes as many as three or four to a village, sometimes only one. Here the peasants draw their water. In villages nearer population centres electricity has been brought to the huts.

At the highest point of the village is the church, usually dilapidated. Today it may be a storehouse or a clubhouse but sometimes still it is a house of worship. Down the hill at the foot of the village there is often a little stream dammed up to provide a duckpond, where the women go to do their laundry.

Inside the huts there may be three or four rooms, usually small and crowded. In the centre, supplying heat for them all, is a large clay stove, on top of which is a shelf where the very old and

very young sleep to keep warm. At the back of the hut live the family's livestock, a cow and perhaps a calf or two, a goat, a few chickens, some ducks and rabbits.

About half of the livestock which supplies Russia's cities with their meat, milk and butter is privately owned and at calving, lambing and kidding time it has the personal care of the peasant's family. Meanwhile the herds owned collectively must survive at the collective mercies of the community.

Behind almost every hut is a fenced-in plot of ground varying from a quarter of an acre to two acres in size, depending on the fertility of the soil. This is the "private plot" which even Stalin could not take away when he forced the peasants into collectives. Here the owner grows vegetables for his family, fodder for his cattle and a few potatoes or cabbages to sell at the nearest provincial town market. On the poorer farms these plots provide a large share of the food and the money the peasant needs to survive, while from the far larger, collectively worked fields surrounding the settlement come the grain and flax and vegetables which the collective is obliged to deliver to the State.

Beyond the village one comes to the only outward signs of the collective system: a cow shed or two for the collectively owned cattle, perhaps a silo and a shed for the farm machinery, and the office building from which a dozen accountants, planners, agricultural experts and the State-appointed chairman rule the farm.

EVEN though they are supervised and regulated by the State, collective farmers do not receive a fixed salary. They work the communal fields with pooled equipment, and at the end of each season they divide the proceeds among themselves according to the amount of work they have performed, though only after the State has taken its prescribed share and after a substantial percentage of the residue is set aside for obligatory capital improvements.

Just how much remains for the peasant is not revealed by the State. That it is certainly nothing to boast about was once indicated by a senior

Soviet agricultural official. "When we are ready to," he said curtly, "we will publish rural income figures." In truth, the collective farms do not produce as much as they should, and this is a source of embarrassment to the Kremlin.

What are the reasons for this inability to expand agriculture? Basically both the czars and the Communists failed because in their mistrust of what they believed to be a "treacherous peasantry" they refused to grant this class the essential freedom and independence which both the Western European peasant and the American farmer have long enjoyed.

IT is no secret to farmers everywhere that their success will always be measured by their willingness and ability to overcome their enemies—frost, drought, unseasonable rains, plant diseases and pests—by adapting the right methods to their needs, and by devoting unlimited hours to gruelling labour unfettered by rules and regulations promulgated by some unseen and perhaps inexperienced master. Nor is it a secret that the most effective compensation for the hardships of farming is the freedom, independence and security that come with owning and tilling one's own plot of land.

Few people have a greater feeling for the soil than the Russian peasantry. It was for this that they were willing to fight innumerable invasions throughout their history and to side with the Bolsheviks in 1917. But the centrally directed agriculture later introduced by the Bolsheviks has none of the conditions and incentives that farmers normally expect. Collective farmers are advised when to plough, what to sow and when to harvest on the collective fields, often without regard to soil conditions and weather. As they are prevented from disposing of their own produce at the best price and as they possess only a tenuous title to the communal land they till, it is little wonder that they neglect the collective farm fields and livestock and concentrate their energies on their tiny private plots and cattle.

Quite apart from this lack of adequate incentives and compensations, the Russian farmer is continually confronted with the inadequacy of the soil itself. A common fallacy held about the Soviet Union is that its vast territory provides it with unlimited arable land. But Russia is relatively poorly endowed with good soil for agriculture. Where the soil is good, as in the famous Black Earth areas of the Ukraine and southern Siberia, rainfall is often uncertain.

In the northern areas, where there is plenty of rain, growing seasons are short, for by far the largest proportion of Russia's arable area lies north of the 45th Parallel. With most of its land area far removed from any water mass, the Soviet Union has great extremes of hot and cold. Hence in many northern areas only the most rapidly maturing grains can be cultivated, and such high-yield grains as winter wheat are limited to the western and southern areas.

Furthermore, great areas in the south-east are semi-arid steppes or sandy deserts where nothing will grow except with irrigation, the installation of which is slow and highly expensive.

WHEN the Bolsheviks seized power in 1917 they had few ideas about how to handle the peasantry's hunger for land. To win support Lenin went along with the slogan of "land to the peasants." But this involved a solution that was non-Marxist, since it would stimulate the growth of tiny capitalist units of family farms.

For a while Lenin, who had no practical experience of agriculture, thought he had found the answer to the peasant problem in rural electrification, which would allow mechanization of many of the farm processes and tend to draw the peasants together into farm communities. But the enormous cost discouraged him.

As food supplies dwindled during the 1920s, other panaceas were eagerly grasped at by the worried leaders in the Kremlin. At one time it was suggested that the meat shortage could be overcome by the mass breeding of rabbits, but diseases and the tendency of rabbits to eat their young caused the project to be abandoned.

Marxist logic dictated that the proper form of agricultural organization should be a State-owned farm or *sovkhoz* on which the workers would receive fixed wages. And indeed such farms were organized after the Revolution. But this system had two drawbacks. In the first place it deprived the peasant of even the thinnest claim to the land—his most treasured possession. Secondly, equipping State farms with machinery required heavy outlays of capital which the government could ill afford. For this reason these farms were considered uneconomical, and their number grew only slowly.

When Stalin came to power slightly more than one per cent of all Russia's cropped arable land was in State farms. The farms were greatly expanded under the first Five-Year Plan, then after a decline grew again. By 1960 the proportion had increased to 30 per cent of total cropland. For one thing, capital was now available to equip them; for another, State farms in some areas could produce grain more cheaply than the collective farms could.

A FORM of agriculture less demanding of the State was the collective farm or *kolkhoz*. Because the *kolkhozes* made use of the already existing livestock, lands and tools of the peasants and presented no labour cost, they required little or no capital outlay by the State. In the first years after the Revolution collectives had not proved popular with the peasants, and their rate of growth was also slow.

During the period of the New Economic Policy in the 1920s, the revival of consumer goods production provided enough inducement to peasants to bring their produce to the cities, for there were things to purchase with the proceeds. But when Stalin decided to push through industrialization in 1929, it was inevitable that consumer industries would suffer and that the incentives to farmers to feed the growing urban labour force would rapidly decline. Somehow a way had to be found of getting cheap foodstuffs to the cities in ever-increasing quantities. Grain was also needed for export from the U.S.S.R. so as to pay for industrial imports.

THE Kremlin's answer was forced collectivization. Tens of thousands of trained party officials were sent to the villages with orders to herd the peasantry into collective farms, by force if necessary. The peasants were divided for this drive into three classes: poor peasants, average peasants and rich peasants or kulaks who possessed livestock and equipment and who employed extra help. Most of the poor and average peasants were persuaded by whatever means were at hand to join the collectives. But the kulaks and many others who clung to their private farms were simply "liquidated as a class" and their possessions confiscated and given to the collectives. Most of them were exiled to Siberia, but many were shot. During the winter of 1929–1930 about one quarter of the peasantry had been herded into collectives, though at incredible cost. Many slaughtered their cattle and horses rather than hand them over. Millions died of starvation or were killed.

Then Stalin put on the brakes, saying the collectivizers were getting "dizzy with success." They must, he cautioned with unparalled hypocrisy, respect the principle of "voluntariness" in making people join collectives. Immediately most of those already collectivized took him at his word and left the *kolkhozes*. But Stalin quickly made it clear that he was not to be taken literally, and within months the deserters were rounded up and forced back into the farms.

Still a few held out in outlying districts. But in the end even the sturdiest resisters were overcome, and by the beginning of 1935 the great majority had been either gathered into the collectives or "liquidated as a class."

The *kolkhozes* were so poorly organized and the peasants so recalcitrant that the harvest of 1932 was far below average. Using brute force, Stalin took what he needed of the crops for the cities and left the peasants to starve. It was probably the worst man-made famine in history. Millions perished in the winter of 1932–1933.

A visitor to the rich Kuban area in 1933 found entire villages utterly deserted. In others a few old women shuffled feebly around their burned-out huts or crawled about the harvested fields collecting chaff which they eagerly munched.

Collectivization had not been designed just to get control of the food supply. Many Communists sincerely believed that by forming large farms suitable for mass cultivation they could greatly increase agricultural production and thereby release large numbers of peasants for work in the rapidly expanding Soviet industries. Thousands of tractors were imported from the West and several factories were built to produce Soviet tractors.

Stalin was too wary, however, to give the tractors directly to the peasants. Instead, he set up machine-tractor stations which for a fee in produce performed all the mechanized cultivating processes. Since the tractor stations actually did the harvesting, they had control of the crops. They took their share, together with the compulsory deliveries for the State, from the first crops to be harvested. If rain or frost delayed the operation, it was the peasants' share that was ruined.

Unfortunately, as with Lenin's electrification and the rabbit-breeding scheme, the high hopes attached to the tractors were also dashed. The tractors themselves were slow in coming. Many were poorly designed and most of the operators were ill-trained. Spare parts were scarce.

It was not an unusual sight in the 1930s to see on a collective farm field a potato seeder pulled by a tractor being driven by a flushed, red-kerchiefed girl. A mechanic would be hanging on to the motor to keep a part functioning and a small boy armed with a hammer would be keeping the pins of the coupling in place, while behind, clinging to the planter, three or four women armed with broom handles would be shoving the potatoes into the ground. Thus half a dozen people would be doing an operation for which one would normally be sufficient.

DURING the 1930s Soviet agricultural production rose considerably. This, however, was due not to greater productivity but to an increase in cultivated areas. During the war years output dropped severely as manpower, horse-power and tractors were drained off by the army. In the postwar years, up to Stalin's death, food production barely kept pace with the growing population.

As in the case of industry, agricultural policy was drastically modified by Stalin's successors. Khrushchev, who even before he rose to the top had concentrated on rural problems, was the first of all the Soviet leaders to have any direct experience with the villages. His first reform was to raise the prices paid to peasants so as to provide an incentive for increasing production.

His second reform was the decentralization of agricultural planning, coupled with the consolidation of collectives into large units. This reduced the number of units from 90,000 to fewer than 60,000. Instead of Moscow's dictating what crops were to be planted where, local authorities were allowed to decide what crops to plant—provided always they delivered the quotas required by the State.

Finally Khrushchev abolished the machine-tractor stations and sold their machines to the farms. With the machines went the drivers and mechanics. Now the farms were able to plan their own agricultural operations without interference from outside organizations.

The abolition of the tractor stations dissipated much of the power Stalin had built up to control the peasantry. However, the consolidation of farms had been accompanied by an expansion of party organizations on each farm, thus assuring Khrushchev the control he needed.

BETTER incentives and the lessening of bureaucratic control caused a temporary increase in agricultural yield, especially in livestock production. But the cities were still not receiving as much meat, butter and milk as Khrushchev had promised.

To fulfill his promises Khrushchev therefore launched a risky programme of ploughing up the semi-arid plains of Kazakhstan and western Siberia. He could grow more grain there and at the same time grow more fodder, mainly corn, in the older agricultural areas of central and south-western Russia. To be sure, the dust bowls of the western United States and Canada were vivid examples of what might happen if one ploughed the light dry soils of the plains, as some Soviet scientists warned. Nevertheless, Khrushchev in 1954 sent the first contingent of hundreds of thousands of young people to the Asiatic steppes to set up State farms.

The move was a calculated risk, and Khrushchev himself stated that even if only three out of five harvests were successful any losses would justify themselves. If his figures are to be believed, however, the first five years produced enough to pay for the entire capital investment and yielded a considerable surplus as well.

However, even some Soviet scientists are still sceptical of the experiment, fearing that two successive years of drought could indeed create dangerous dust bowls. Today trained agricultural experts supervise most ploughing operations, especially in marginal terrain, and constant efforts are being made to retain the heavy winter snows on the fields so as to provide the additional moisture needed in the spring growing season.

THE Kazakhstan experiment, according to experts, has used up the last available land in the Soviet Union that is even marginally suitable for cultivation. If the Kremlin hopes to give every Soviet citizen an adequately balanced diet in the future it will have to find some way of intensifying the cultivation of existing arable land by better methods and by greater use of fertilizers. That this fact is realized by the Kremlin is indicated by the threefold increase planned for Soviet chemical production during the recently inaugurated Seven-Year Plan. The plan envisages not only more fertilizers but the manufacture of plastics as substitutes for some of the land's inadequate commercial agricultural products such as flax and leather.

The agricultural reforms since Stalin's death have probably put an end to the hand-to-mouth existence which Russia has led for the past century. It is another question whether these artificial incentives and improvements have proved a viable substitute for the initiative of the individual farmer, which in other countries, notably the United States, has produced not just sufficiency but over-abundance.

*On a farm near Alma-Ata a farm worker gathers hay, typifying the primitive methods that are still widely practised in the U.S.S.R.*

# Struggle to Produce More Food

The desperate attempt of the Kremlin over the past four decades to increase Soviet agricultural yield has taken place on a land that is in large part poor for crops. While some areas are ideal for growing a wide variety of grains and other produce, others are only marginally useful and a great many are unfit for·cultivation. The disparity, combined with the widespread lack of modern farming methods and poor climatic conditions in many regions, has given extra drama and pathos to the Kremlin's relentless drive to organize the country's peasants for greater production.

77

COLLECTIVE FARMS *are centred around rural villages which are organized as a single economic unit. After the State has taken its share of the produce, the rest of the crops and the money earned are divided among the peasants*

MECHANICAL SEEDERS are examples of modern farm machinery which is gradually becoming more prevalent on Russia's farms. Such equipment, once operated by government units, is now the property of the collectives.

FARM VILLAGE STREET near Lake Baikal in Siberia shows how collective farms are arranged. Peasants can grow crops for themselves on plots at the back of their houses but the large fields beyond are collectively owned.

SWEEPING WHEAT on a collective near the Kazakhstan border, teenage farm girls use home-made twig brooms to pile up the newly harvested grain for cleaning. Later the grain will be dried, then stored in barns.

*Sugar beet is shovelled into large mounds by farmers on a collective farm in Uzbekistan which earns £130,000 a year*

POURING MILK. Women care for a herd of cattle on a collective farm not far from Moscow. The milkmaid at right marks down each cow's production in a notebook.

FARM BOUNTY *from the soil is ample in some areas, particularly in European Russia with its gently rolling steppe, but also in the new cotton-producing region of Soviet Central Asia*

CENTRAL ASIAN COTTON PICKERS wearing native skull-caps pile their yield on a wagon. This is in the Fergana Valley, one of the world's oldest cultivated regions.

Good soil and a warm climate enable Central Asian farmers to grow 90 per cent of all Soviet cotton. Total cotton yield in Russia is about half of that of the United States.

ANTIQUATED COMBINE with a two-man crew harvests wheat on a vast State farm of the kind that is now spreading over Siberia. Russian workers have impressed Western agricultural experts with the skill with which they operate their equipment. Though some of the machinery is as old-fashioned as that above, most of it is reliable and well built.

STATE FARMS, *owned outright by the government, are manned by peasants who work for a fixed wage. Though less numerous than the collective farms, such units are growing in importance*

COUNTRY SHOP on a State farm near the Central Asian city of Alma-Ata indicates the spartan surroundings of these units, whose inhabitants live as in a military camp.

EXHIBITION HALL in Moscow (*right*), where livestock and farm machinery are exhibited, is one of many where Russian farmers are shown how to improve output.

**FOOD DISTRIBUTION** *is only slowly being modernized.*
*Consumers can usually buy nothing but perishables*
*grown locally, since refrigerated transport is scarce*

IN A GEORGIAN MARKET in Tbilisi men and women from collective farms sell grapes. The rich wines of mountainous Georgia are highly prized throughout Russia.

SHOPPING FOR VEGETABLES in a Moscow free market, a girl buys cabbage. Farmers from the Moscow area bring surplus produce here and charge what the customers will pay.

A MIDDLE-CLASS FARMER,
Ivan Teslenko joins his wife
in preparing an evening meal
in their home outside Kiev.
A collective farm chairman,
he is government-appointed.

# Classes
# in a Classless
# Society

DESPITE Marx's promises of a classless society, and despite the Bolshevik liquidation
first of the Russian aristocracy, then of the
bourgeoisie and finally of the successful small
farmers or kulaks, class distinctions in the Soviet
Union are becoming more marked with each
passing year.

Marx and his disciples believed that class divisions were based on the ownership of the means of
production. If private ownership could be done

away with, classes would disappear. But as the
Yugoslav ex-Communist Milovan Djilas has
pointed out, it is not ownership of production
that counts, but control. Like the managers of
Western industry today, the directors of Soviet
industries do not own their factories but they do
effectively control them, and with control come
the perquisites and privileges on which modern
classes are founded. As a result of these perquisites
and privileges the new Soviet upper classes are

87

able to pass on to their children their accumulated wealth, cultural tastes, intellectual aspirations and educational opportunities and thereby help perpetuate their class.

In its present stage of development Soviet society is still more flexible than many of the older societies of western Europe. The average young Russian today has many opportunities of rising from humble origins to affluence, perhaps more than his counterpart does in most other modern States. But the opportunities of climbing up the Soviet ladder—and the chances of falling down it—are steadily diminishing.

Because of the reticence of Soviet statisticians, it is almost impossible to draw precise lines between classes on the basis of income. The best one can do is to examine a case or two in each of the major categories into which Soviet society seems to break down.

IN the very shadow of one of the gaudy skyscrapers with which Stalin adorned Moscow stands a high, unpainted fence. Through an open gateway one can see a long wooden barrack-like building standing in a sea of mud. Slippery planks laid across the mud lead to the door. Inside are a series of cubicles perhaps 10 feet square and separated from one another by flimsy partitions. In each of these cubicles there is a bed, a chair or two and perhaps a table. At the end of the building are individual oil burners, a table and a few shelves on which the occupants keep their cooking and eating utensils. Outside behind the building there is an outhouse, and in front there is a water tap that is wrapped to prevent the inhabitants' water supply from freezing during the winter.

The building was erected in 1930 during the first Five-Year Plan, to provide temporary housing for the unskilled labourers who were swarming into the cities from the villages. Stalin promised that by the end of a couple of Five-Year Plans there would be permanent housing for everyone. But the promise never came true and the building is still serving its original purpose.

In the daytime the rooms are empty, for the men and women are at work and the children are at school or in a nursery. Around seven p.m. a

mother—let us call her Lydia—returns from the cafeteria in which she works as a waitress, bringing her two-year-old son, whom she has picked up at a State-run nursery. Half an hour later her husband, Yuri, an unskilled construction worker, trudges into the cubicle. He brings with him a small parcel containing some bread and sausage and a bottle filled with milk. He had taken the bottle to work in the morning and had managed to get it filled, following work, after standing in a queue for half an hour.

LEAVING the child with Yuri, Lydia makes her way through the other cubicles to the kitchen. Half a dozen other women are already there, and Lydia waits until she can find room to prepare some milk and food for the child.

When the meal is ready she feeds the baby and puts him to bed in a home-made cot next to the bed. Then she and Yuri eat a cold supper of bread, sausage and perhaps an apple. The meal is not very appetizing but they do not mind, for they have both had a hot mid-day meal at their places of work.

Occasionally Yuri and Lydia treat themselves to a film, but otherwise their recreation is confined to visiting friends, strolling in the Park of Culture and Rest, or window-shopping in Gorky Street on Sundays and holidays.

Yuri earns just over £5 a week. Lydia earns £4 at her waitress job—slightly more than the legal minimum wage. The two wages add up to £9 a week, about the minimum on which a family of three can live—which explains why almost every woman in the Soviet Union works. Out of the £9, Yuri and Lydia spend about £6 on food: a pound or two of beef every week, bread, margarine, tea, potatoes, a few vegetables, milk and very little sugar.

Almost all the rest of the family income is spent on clothing, and not very much of it either, because shirts cost £2. 5s., suits £65, shoes £8 and rayon dresses £12. As a result both Yuri and Lydia wear light, inexpensive sandals in summer and rubber boots in winter. Each of them has a shabby overcoat, but the baby has a heavy imitation fur coat and fur hat. Yuri and Lydia feel, as do most Russian parents, that the children come first.

Rent is surprisingly low for Yuri and Lydia. The charge, based on a few pence per square yard per month, presents no problem inasmuch as the whole family occupies only a few square yards. Doctors' bills are also no problem because medical care, when available, is free. Foreign doctors returning from Russia agree that Soviet medical research and scientific knowledge are of a high order. But in practice, as the Soviet Press constantly complains, medical care is less than adequate. Though almost all the new drugs available in the West are also produced in Russia, the supply is so limited that unless one can afford a private doctor (*i.e.*, one who is engaged in private practice in addition to his State duties) or knows someone in the pharmaceutical industry, many of the commonest drugs are unavailable.

For example, although medicines for tuberculosis are manufactured in Russia, they are so difficult to obtain that this disease is still widespread outside the big cities.

SOVIET medical students say privately that the frequent mental disorders among poorer people are brought about largely by overcrowding and lack of privacy. Lack of good housing has also been blamed for the recent slackening off in the Russian birth rate.

Perhaps the most prevalent "disease" among the working class, however, is sheer boredom, and the commonest medicine for this is vodka. But the State has set the price of vodka so high that the workers must do without it or brew their own.

Soviet statistics give no indication of the size of this lowest class. It may be taken to include all those people who earn less than £32 a month, which is the average wage of urban workers in the U.S.S.R. today. But it has been estimated that more than half the entire Soviet population is in this wage group.

How do Yuri and Lydia, who find themselves at the very bottom of the social ladder, reconcile their plight with the Communist regime's long-standing promises of paradise? Few if any of the barrack-dwellers are members of the party or even of the Komsomol, for if they were they would long since have acquired better quarters and better jobs. Yuri's schooling is finished, and because only a better education could assure him of substantial future advancement he has little hope of rising appreciably above his present level.

Yuri and Lydia both recognize, however, that living conditions have been improving perceptibly in the past few years. With enough to eat, they already have something to lose, and though they grumble over their lot and have no love for the regime, their minds are preoccupied with the problems of daily living.

Furthermore, as Russian citizens they have an exaggerated feeling of reverence for and pride in their country, and though they may resent the priority of rockets over shoes they derive some solace from their association with Soviet technological and scientific accomplishments. Toward the regime itself, their reaction is principally one of apathy and resignation, tempered with the self-abasement reflected in the ancient peasant saying: "We are a dark people."

ON a side street near the Kremlin the attention of a passer-by is attracted by the sound of singing, which rises from a ventilator at the edge of the pavement. It is the evening of November 7, the Soviet national holiday. Through the grating the passer-by sees a window 10 feet below street level, opening onto the ventilator. In the semi-basement room within, a naked bulb lights up a table set for the great annual holiday dinner of cold ham, sardines, margarine, bread, cheese, cucumber and potato salad. A small, half-empty carafe of vodka sits on the table, together with a bottle of sweet red wine. On an oil stove in the corner a tin of goulash is warming, and its strong smell rises through the ventilator. Two couples are seated around the table, and beside them a small child is asleep on the double-decked bed.

In low voices the two couples are singing an old Russian song that is as deep and mournful as a dirge. Their faces are solemn and as sad as the song. At the end of the song the men pour themselves some vodka, the women some wine. They toast one another gravely, take a bite of food and sing again, desperately determined to enjoy themselves.

The occupants of this subterranean room are one rung up the ladder from the couple in the barrack-building. The host, whom we may call Stepan, is a government clerk and earns up to £12 a week. His wife Natasha is a secretary and earns £8 a week. The banquet before them does not reflect these salaries, for the Russian's pride and sense of hospitality dictate that when he celebrates he must turn his pockets inside out and leave them empty until the next payday comes along to enable him to refill them.

Stepan and other clerks like him, foremen, technicians and skilled workers who are paid between £10 and £25 a week represent perhaps 30 to 40 per cent of the urban wage earners of the Soviet Union. In a way Stepan and Natasha are better off than many others in their income group, for they live in Moscow, only a stone's throw from the Kremlin, the centre of their universe.

Yet their room is damp and dark. No sunlight ever reaches it through the ventilator in the pavement. It is one of four rooms in the basement flat. Each of the other rooms is occupied by a family like theirs. All share a tiny kitchen that supplements the oil stoves they keep in their rooms. A single bathroom and a single toilet serve a dozen people. The dark corridor connecting the rooms is cluttered with trunks, boxes, bundles of old clothing and sacks of potatoes. The air is musty and smells of sweat, bad drains and wet overcoats.

But the apartment's most critical area is the common kitchen, particularly in the evenings when the four housewives, tired after a day's work and an hour's shopping, try to cook their separate suppers over the small wood-burning stove. In the corridor outside the kitchen a printed

**STEPAN AND NATASHA'S FAMILY BUDGET**

| | |
|---|---|
| Food | £40 |
| Clothing | £16 |
| Rent, fuel etc. | £3 |
| Recreation, durable goods | £10 |
| Income tax | £5 |
| Miscellaneous | £6 |
| **Total** | **£70** |

MONTHLY EXPENSES are shown for a family with two wage earners. Durable goods include house supplies. The income tax will disappear by 1965, but a big sales tax will continue to be levied.

notice entitled "Rules for Communal Living" has been posted in an attempt to foresee and forestall the endless disputes and frictions which such conditions must give rise to.

One rule states that chopping wood in the corridors is forbidden. Another categorically prohibits draining off water from the radiators to make tea. The rules establish a system of priorities for the use of the kitchen stove and they also warn the flat dwellers against actions that might grate on their neighbours' nerves—playing musical instruments after midnight, hogging the stove, or behaving in an unsocial manner.

When, as happens too often, disputes do break out, order is to be restored by the house manager, a glorified caretaker who may serve four or five apartment houses with perhaps a thousand tenants. If he fails, a recently instituted extra-legal "Comradely Court," composed of tenants selected by the building's senior party members, can put the offenders on trial. The court can levy minor fines or it can even recommend to the police that the troublemakers' residence permits for Moscow—perhaps their most precious privilege —be rescinded, forcing them to move to the provinces.

In addition to the children, the families in these flats frequently include grandparents, who are convenient as baby-sitters and can spend their free hours in a queue to buy milk, oil or other scarce items. But because space is limited they frequently must sleep on the boxes and trunks in the corridors.

Like Yuri and Lydia, Stepan and Natasha allot the major share of their family budget to food. They do have a little more left over for clothes, but not much for entertainment. The guests they are entertaining are a young doctor and his wife, who because of the husband's professional status consider themselves members of Russia's intelligentsia. But when the doctor looks at his shabby suit he complains to Natasha, "How can anyone belong to the intelligentsia in a suit like this? And how can one have anything better on £9 a week?"

Occasionally Stepan and Natasha can afford a film or even the theatre but generally they spend their evenings in their cellar flat reading. Russians are voracious readers and it does not cost much to get a book from one of the bookshops.

EVEN though their life and surroundings are drab and dreary, Stepan and Natasha will tell you that things are better than ever before. In contrast to the situation a few years ago the shops of Moscow today are full of things to buy. These things are as yet too expensive for their means, but they fervently hope they will soon be able to afford not only suits but a television set and a sewing machine, and perhaps one day some of the gadgets in the dream kitchens Natasha has seen in foreign exhibitions in Moscow.

But what encourages them most are the acres of new housing springing up in the suburbs. The lack of adequate housing has long evoked the Russian people's bitterest complaints, not merely in Moscow and other big cities but in the smaller provincial towns and new industrial communities beyond the Urals, where for many years people have occupied space scarcely larger than the beds they sleep in.

Russia's housing shortage was not acute until the 1930s. During the early years of the Communist regime many city dwellers had gone back to the villages in search of food. But when Stalin started his industrial drive in 1929 the cities were flooded with new workers. Moscow's population grew from a million and a half to five million in a single generation.

Although Stalin did put up some buildings in the larger cities, this did not begin to provide adequate space for the new workers. The crowding became so severe that after Stalin's death his successors quickly sought a remedy.

The first post-Stalin attempts were only half-hearted, and they were bogged down in the general shortage of housing materials brought about by the priority given to heavy industry. Not until Khrushchev turned to the problem in

1956 was any real headway made. Ordering an end to all fanciful architectural designs, Khrushchev instructed his engineers to devise techniques for mass housing production. Today great square grey blocks of flats made of concrete slabs are springing up in all large Soviet cities just as quickly as the cement can be made and the slabs poured.

The buildings themselves are ugly and the flats within are a far cry from the modern housing one sees in Europe. Door handles come off in one's hands, windows fail to close, electric wiring is faulty, floors buckle and walls crack a few weeks after they are finished.

Yet for all these defects the new buildings represent the height of ambition for the tenants of the barracks and basements and ancient, crowded buildings where most urban dwellers live today. For regardless of their shoddy construction they provide what Russians today long for more than anything else: privacy.

THE lack of privacy has been blamed not only for an increase in nervous disorders but also for the present high Soviet divorce rate. Jammed into cramped quarters, families have got on one another's nerves to such an extent that children have left their parents and the parents have left each other.

The longing for privacy is nowhere more apparent than in the communities of new private houses which are sprouting up on the outskirts of most of the smaller cities of Russia. When Khrushchev launched his housing drive, he encouraged private initiative by instructing city councils to allocate plots to private home builders and ordering industry to provide the necessary building materials. In many towns the response was so great that private housing was soon going up almost as fast as government-subsidized flats. And the first thing most of the private builders put up was a high wooden fence around their plot.

Inevitably, enterprising racketeers have taken advantage of the new dispensation by building houses with huge rooms which they then subdivide and rent out, thus in effect becoming a latter-day variety of the extortionate landlords against whom the Bolsheviks had revolted in 1917. Others have become building contractors, erecting bungalows under assumed names and selling them to the highest bidder. While the Communist authorities will doubtless have little difficulty in liquidating the new class of landlords whenever they so desire, the building racketeers have demonstrated the irrepressibility of private enterprise and initiative after more than four decades of Communism.

In contrast to the members of Russia's lower class, who are so apathetic, the clerks and technicians of the lower middle class are stirring with the expectations that have been provoked by Khrushchev's promises of a better deal. Already the slight improvements they have experienced are giving rise to hopes of more.

JUST across the river from the Kremlin near the Stone Bridge rises a large concrete block of flats in the severe style of the late 1920s. Once a light grey, the porous cement of which it was made has absorbed three decades of Moscow soot and is now an ugly black, unwashable and unpaintable, a dreary reminder of Stalin's one excursion into functional architecture. This is the Dom Pravitelstva, the House of the Government. It was built to house the favoured members of the Soviet hierarchy after Stalin, denouncing egalitarianism, had declared that high officials should enjoy the comforts commensurate with their station.

The tenants of the Dom once included such prominent men as Nikolai Bukharin, the last of Stalin's major rivals to be killed; Karl Radek, the propagandist who is presumed to have died after many years of exile in eastern Siberia, and a dozen other Old Bolsheviks. Its current tenants, however, feel more secure in their occupancy. Although many of the newer blocks of flats are more luxurious and spacious, the Dom is still the original home of the upper middle class.

Its flats have several rooms and are usually occupied not by a small tribe of children, grandparents and country cousins but by the immediate family of a successful writer, artist or party functionary. Some of the flats are penthouses, while others boast large balconies overlooking the Kremlin and the Moskva River. Most have a full complement of servants—cooks, maids and nursemaids.

THE Soviet upper middle class consists today of top industrial managers and factory directors, leading engineers, senior military officers, popular novelists and artists, university professors and members of the Academy of Sciences. Their incomes vary between £2,000 and £4,000 a year and can go as high as £10,000. Altogether they probably comprise less than 10 per cent of the country's population.

Most of the members of this group maintain *dachas* and many actually own them. The *dacha* is a peculiarly Russian institution which reflects the strong attachment of almost every Russian to the soil, the forest and nature. Probably millions of city dwellers go each summer "to the *dacha*." It may be a room just big enough for a bed in a tumble-down hut, or it may be a large stone villa complete with billiard room and conservatory and situated in a wooded park, with a boat house and a speedboat on a lake or the Moskva River. Owners of these sumptuous villas, if they do not own a car, may have the use of a chauffeur-driven car from the factory or institute at which they work.

Many of them also take holidays on the Black Sea coast, where if they do not have a villa themselves, they take de luxe accommodations at the better hotels and sanatoriums along the coast.

Because they hold influential positions in the party, on the production side of the economy or in other areas of great importance to the State, many of them live better than their salaries would indicate. Among the benefits they enjoy is the opportunity to accept goods and services in exchange for the political favours which they can dispense.

For the most part risen from modest surroundings, the upper middle class in Russia has a passion for culture. These are the people who fill the thirty-odd theatres of Moscow and the hundreds of provincial theatres and opera houses every night of the week. They compete with one another in buying whatever modern paintings the young artists of Moscow produce and some even spend huge sums buying what few relics of the old aristocracy are still left in the antique shops of Moscow and Leningrad: Meissen china, old jewellery, Fabergé enamels and porcelain Easter eggs.

Much of their income goes on their wardrobes, for like the newly rich everywhere they are painfully self-conscious of their appearance. To buy a few yards of French dress material or English suiting at GUM (a big department store) on Red Square, or on a trip abroad, they will spend half a month's salary. They will spend another half having it made up into a dress or suit by one of the few good tailors in town.

BUT probably their most serious concern is their children. Many of them started life as manual workers, and they abhor the thought that their children may have to work again as labourers. Knowing that a university education is the only road to jobs as good as theirs, they go to great lengths to assure their children's entrance into the crowded universities. Often they employ private tutors to prepare their sons for the stiff entrance examinations. Occasionally they resort to pressure or even outright bribery of college officials in order to have their children accepted. In fact the resistance of parents to their children undertaking manual labour has been cited by Khrushchev himself as one of the main reasons for recent radical reforms being made in the educational system (see Chapter 7).

A small minority among the adults of this class may dream of an increase in spiritual rather than material rewards and may long for such imponderables as freedom of self-expression, but the concern of the materialistic majority is to avoid losing the means that have brought them to such affluence. In sharp contrast to the adventurous, dedicated older party leaders who originally conquered Russia for Communism and who still entertain the vision of conquering the world, the upper middle class is bent on keeping things as they are and avoiding adventures both at home and abroad.

ON the high right bank of the Moskva River in south-west Moscow, in an area once known as Sparrow Hills and now called Lenin Hills, are five stately white mansions. Across the river is the Luzhniki Sports Park, and beyond it in the distance are the towers of the Kremlin. Each of the mansions stands on a large site surrounded by a high fence. One lane of the two-way road behind the houses is closed to traffic, and ordinarily a uniformed policeman can be seen patrolling the pavement.

Just who it is that occupies these houses at any given moment is a constant source of speculation to politically-minded Muscovites. But there is no doubt what group the occupants represent. They are men at the pinnacle of the Soviet regime: high-ranking members of the party Presidium or the Council of Ministers.

The salary of a Soviet leader is not public knowledge, and it is not very important. In the early days after the Revolution the party leaders deliberately limited their incomes to relatively low amounts. But since these leaders are supplied with cars and chauffeurs, probably with household staffs and certainly with special housing, their cash salaries are secondary.

Furthermore most of them draw huge sums from the publication of their "literary works." These are often no more than collections of their speeches, but they are published in editions of hundreds of thousands of copies and are required reading for the party membership. Royalties from such editions can run to extremely high figures.

Sharing the privileged status of the party leaders and government Ministers,—though not their power—are a handful of senior scientists, writers, artists and leading generals, many of whom are highly paid. Together they comprise only a tiny fraction of one per cent of the population. They are the cream of the cream.

In addition to their flats in Moscow and their luxuriously appointed *dachas*—occasionally a single family has several—many of this privileged group maintain expensive villas on the Black Sea. Stalin used to reward leading personalities by giving them a seaside house, often one suddenly vacated when the dictator liquidated its owner. But now these villas have been confiscated and are allocated to government or party leaders for temporary use according to their political importance.

Since the war a favourite resort for the very wealthy is Karlovy Vary (formerly Carlsbad) in Czechoslovakia. Before the second World War many of the most prominent of Europe's aristocracy went there to "take the cure" at the end of the social season. Today, where once kings and emperors congregated, leading Soviet actors, dancers and writers bask in new-found luxury.

MEMBERSHIP in this group today is as exclusive as high society in Western capitals ever been. The luxurious standard of living and high connections of its members tend to keep them aloof from even the rich managers and professors of the upper middle class. Occasionally they may take in a rising young engineer much as the smart circles of London or New York might adopt and lionize a young poet. But generally they keep to themselves, even to the extent of marrying within the confines of the group.

Income taxes have never been higher than 13 per cent in Soviet Russia and are now being abolished, so that the elite can look forward to keeping most of their money. Though Marx inveighed against inherited wealth, there is no inheritance tax in the Soviet Union beyond a simple probate fee. Thus the very rich can guarantee that their children will also be rich.

*Dacha* parties, dancing and record-collecting are the chief preoccupations of the younger members of the group, although all of them are required to safeguard their status as "useful citizens" by enrolling in some educational institute. From time to time the debauchery and orgies of these younger people, who are known as the "jet set," lead to crimes and scandals. But these seldom reach the pages of the Press.

THE stratification of Russia's society into classes has never been part of the Kremlin's plan for building Socialism. On the contrary, it has taken place as the unavoidable consequence of a society's rising from poverty and want, and it has occurred, at least in the upper strata, against the better judgment of old Communists who have always sought the classless society.

One reason it has occurred is that more than in any Western country, children in Russia occupy the place of privilege. Even the poorest parent tends to lavish what small possessions he has on his sons and daughters. And in the upper classes, the determination of parents to give their children the advantages they as children of the Revolution were denied has been stronger than any Kremlin decree that has been thus far promulgated.

The political effect which the hardening of class divisions is having upon the ideological purity of the Soviet State is of deep concern to the party leaders—even though their own families are among the most prominent beneficiaries of the development. Twice in recent times the Kremlin leaders have warned that the desire for higher living standards must not diminish the national effort to expand Soviet and Communist power. But there seems to be no stopping the formation of classes in a classless society.

*During an evening party 10-year-old Evgeny Dmitriev dances Cossack-style with his father's employer. Behind Evgeny is his mother*

# A Brighter Prospect for living

Long accustomed to a bleak existence, the people of Russia in the past few years have witnessed a considerable improvement in general living conditions. More and better housing accommodation and the gradual increase in the availability of consumer goods have noticeably brightened family life. By Western standards, however, the average Russian's lot is still a limited one. Even a well-situated family like the Alexei Dmitrievs, shown above and on the next two pages, feel they are fortunate to be able to rent a cramped three-and-a-half-room Leningrad flat.

**FAMILY PARTY** brings together the Dmitrievs and two other couples on a Saturday night. Serafima Dmitriev is at the far left, her husband Alexei second from the right. On the far right is young Evgeny. Proposing a toast is Alexei Chantsev, Dmitriev's boss at the Stalin Metal Works in Leningrad. The Dmitrievs have two other sons, both

## a skilled worker and party member

BOOK CABINET, which by day hides the boys' folding beds, prominently displays the biography of Lenin, a dark-covered volume in the middle of the second shelf.

WASHING DISHES in the kitchen sink, Serafima Dmitriev uses a sink that provides only cold water. Kitchen equipment includes an electric iron and an electric teapot.

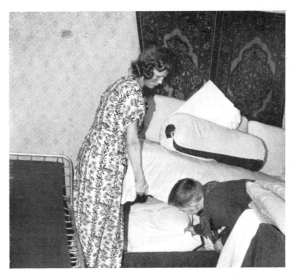

teenagers, but both of them were out that evening. The five Dmitrievs—husband, wife and three sons—occupy their one-bedroom Leningrad flat for £2. 5s. a month.

MAKING UP BEDS, Serafima and Evgeny get pillows and sheets which are stored during the day. The three boys sleep in the bedroom, the parents in the living-room.

*In a Ukrainian village shop a peasant couple contemplate a purchase. The abacus on the right will be used to work out the price*

SHOPPING *for non-essential products is still a*
*relatively novel experience. Consumer goods remain scarce*
*and expensive, but their existence in both city and*
*country shops has given people a window to another world*

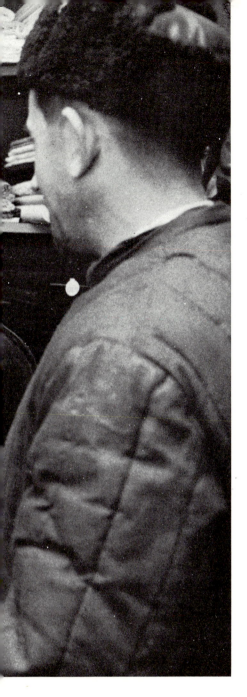

BIGGEST STORE in Moscow, GUM (whose initials stand for State Department Store), was once an arcade for private shops. An office building under Stalin, it was reopened as a store after his death.

CROWDED BRIDGE carries shoppers at GUM across the sky-lighted arcade. GUM is packed with people from Moscow and nearby communities every evening and on Sundays and holidays.

WINDOW SHOPPERS gaze at the latest fashions as shown by GUM. Few can afford these clothes, but the increased availability of goods gives the Russian people a special incentive to continue striving.

# A BETTER EXISTENCE

*seems more attainable today
than it did under Stalin, with
higher wages in the factories,
better prices for farm products
and, above all, new houses
which begin to satisfy
the great longing for privacy*

PRIVATE HOUSING, as on a hillside in Volsk on the Volga River (*below*), is mostly privately built. The State lends up to £400 at two per cent interest for new houses or improvement.

CHILDREN in the Soviet Union are the first to receive the benefits of any increase in living standards. Here a child, bundled against the winter cold, pushes a sledge.

SOURCE OF PRIDE for Russians is the world-famous Moscow underground. Begun in 1932, it is constantly being enlarged. It is clean and comfortable, rarely gets too over-crowded.

COUNCIL FLATS, newly built on the outskirts of Moscow (*below*), have lost the ornate style of Stalin's day. Buildings are mass-produced and built of concrete.

# 7

# The Schooling of Soviet Thought

NEAR the entrance to the Park of Culture and Rest in Stalinabad, in a far corner of the Soviet Union, a young man is standing on a small wooden platform. Before him a dozen or so strollers have stopped to listen, but most of the people glance at him and move on to watch a team of high-wire acrobats, or to listen to a jazz band in a little outdoor theatre.

The young man—fair-haired, good-looking and obviously from European Russia—is speaking vigorously and well. You might think he was a quack advertising some patent medicine at a fairground, but the product he is selling is not a bottled cure-all. It is Communism, and at the moment he is explaining the latest crimes of the capitalist nations, particularly the United States. When he pauses for a moment an onlooker asks a question, and the speaker patiently answers it. Another question follows and again the young man gives the official answer.

The young man is a representative of Agitprop, the Communist Party Bureau for Agitation (the spoken word) and Propaganda (the written word). Agitprop is responsible for guiding public opinion in the Soviet Union.

One of the most widespread misconceptions about Russia is that public opinion plays no role in the Kremlin's political calculations. On the contrary, the leaders pay as much attention to what people are thinking as a wise military leader pays to the morale of his troops. For while public opinion in the Soviet Union, like morale in an army, does not guide policies or encourage initiative as it sometimes does in the West, it does determine the degree of enthusiasm with which the population performs the tasks given to it and the degree of acquiescence with which it accepts the Kremlin's policies.

The Agitprop man in the park is both a speaker and an assessor of public opinion. When he returns to party headquarters he will prepare a detailed report on the frame of mind of his listeners, the questions they ask and their reactions to the answers—anything that will help his superiors gauge the state of public opinion at the moment.

AS the Communists began to consolidate their control after 1917, they recognized that to preserve themselves in power they would have to do more than propagate the party line to the masses. They would also have to prevent anyone else from spreading a different view. From the start they closely supervised all public communication. They screened and increasingly prohibited foreign newspapers, books and films, and at the same time censored all publications within the country. In Stalin's later days nearly all public communication with the outside world was stopped, and after the second World War a great effort was made to prevent foreign broadcasts from reaching the Russian people.

Stalin's successors have relaxed these measures to some degree and have permitted contact with the outside world through tourism and cultural- and scientific-exchange programmes. But even today political ideas not consonant with Communist doctrine are strictly suppressed.

The ultimate aim of the Soviet propaganda effort is to develop the New Soviet Man: the hero of Socialism, free of all capitalist or bourgeois "prejudices," who will happily and unselfishly produce according to his abilities and consume according to his needs. This is also one of the principal goals of Soviet education. Both Lenin and Stalin recognized that the first prerequisite for a politically sound public state of mind was education. Before the Revolution 65 per cent of all Russia's citizens had been illiterate, and one of the first campaigns launched by the Bolsheviks was "the battle to stamp out illiteracy." The drive was remarkably successful: except among older people, illiteracy today is almost non-existent in the U.S.S.R.

STALIN himself had another compelling reason for improving public education. If he was to realize his hopes of making Russia into a modern industrial nation, he could not depend on foreign technicians indefinitely but would have to develop his own pool of experts. Schools and universities were organized not to produce well-educated men and women but to turn out engineers to build and operate the economy. Today they produce a far higher proportion of engineers than does the United States.

Except for the children of very highly placed citizens, every young Russian knows that his entire future depends on his education. Anyone who stops his education at the end of the required eight years of schooling knows that he will never rise above the ranks of unskilled labour. The eleven-year-schoolboy may rise another rung. The trade-school product rises further, but unless he possesses a university diploma he can never get to the top of the ladder no matter how hard he works or how able he is. Thus with rare exceptions the Soviet self-made man is made in school and at the universities. As a result, learning occupies an even higher place of honour, both with authorities and with students, than it does in countries of the West.

From the primary school to university level, tuition today is free. Most university students receive living allowances or grants according to their academic standing and the subjects they are studying. Grants are raised when it is necessary to attract students into certain professions, and lowered to discourage entrance into non-essential professions. The number permitted to study for a given profession is determined by official esti-

### WHO GOES TO SCHOOL

|  | U.S.S.R. | U.S. |
|---|---|---|
| **School attendance: Children** | | |
| Primary level | 29,500,000 | 33,400,000 |
| Secondary level | 9,000,000 | 9,000,000 |
| Higher educational institutions | 2,500,000 | 3,700,000 |
| **School completion: Adults** | | |
| Did not complete primary level | 52,000,000 | 21,600,000 |
| Completed primary level only | 34,500,000 | 33,900,000 |
| Completed secondary level only | 19,500,000 | 34,000,000 |
| Graduated from higher institutions | 3,800,000 | 7,600,000 |

EDUCATIONAL LEVEL of the Soviet people is compared to that of the U.S. population. All figures are estimates, and adults are those who are 25 and over. Despite a smaller population, the U.S. has more children in elementary school and at the university level. A larger proportion of Americans than Russians attend secondary school, principally because most State laws require children to stay in school two years longer than children must in Russia.

mates of the number of graduates the profession will need.

As a result Soviet students do not have the free choice of future career that Europeans have. Many students, for example, hope to go into journalism, perhaps because they believe it will give them an opportunity to travel and see the world. But the need for journalists is limited. Hence grants for journalism students are low and vacancies in journalism courses few. But grants and vacancies for mining students are high because the mining profession has been in need of skilled engineers for many years.

In the early years of the Soviet regime there was much experimenting with progressive methods of education. Formal examinations were few, classroom discipline was lax and students were even encouraged to criticize their teachers. But Stalin, who was himself educated in a Tbilisi seminary, was unimpressed by these methods and ordered a return to the most conservative teaching practices. Today Soviet schools and universities are characterized by the strictest discipline, by frequent tests and by a paternalistic attitude in the determination of courses and curricula. Foreign educationalists have often criticized the rigidity of the system, arguing that it stifles individual student initiative.

Four years of schooling was made obligatory for all children soon after 1917. Subsequently this was raised to seven years, although this goal was never fully realized in some rural and outlying districts. Today an eight-year course is obligatory, after which most Soviet children either go to work or attend trade schools. A small proportion at this crucial point are selected for three years of secondary or grammar-school-level study and, if they are not subsequently weeded out, for the pinnacle of their ambitions: a university education.

Little political indoctrination takes place at the primary level, except for the slogans that constantly dog the life of every Soviet citizen. But systematic emphasis on Communist theory and practice is a feature of secondary-school history and civics courses. Most Soviet secondary education is given in ordinary day schools, although correspondence courses are extensively used in the upper grades, especially for technical instruction. In recent years, however, a system of boarding schools has been inaugurated by the Kremlin. These provide an especially good opportunity for the State to indoctrinate the young in Communist dogma.

MOST children between nine and fourteen belong to the Pioneers, an organization something like the Scouts in Western countries. Almost every community has its Pioneer Palace where the young are taught singing, dancing, camping and other activities. On entrance they take a solemn oath "to love the Soviet Union, to live, to study, and to fight according to the teachings of Lenin and . . . the Communist

Party." The Pioneers give the Russian child his first real taste of Communist regimentation.

During the summer many of the young go to Pioneer camps. Visitors to the Bratsk hydro-electric project several hundred miles north of Irkutsk in the Siberian wilderness may go by motorboat down the Angara River into the Siberian forest, where on a small backwater they will find a dock decorated with banners proclaiming the Bratsk Pioneer Camp.

Above the dock a hundred Pioneers in shorts and white shirts, with triangular red kerchiefs neatly tied around their necks, are lined up. At a word from their commander they break into a stirring song of welcome. Later, they show their visitors the barracks and mess hall, the open air theatre and finally their fondest possession: two bear cubs which a local hunter caught in the forest nearby. These Pioneers are children of the workers at Bratsk.

BETWEEN the ages of 15 and 18 a large number of Pioneers enter the next level of political activity, the Komsomol or Communist Youth Organization. Here they are subjected to more intense political indoctrination, and some undertake special tasks for the State like spreading party propaganda or opening up new lands for agriculture. The Komsomol is the testing ground for subsequent membership in the Communist party.

Out of the million and a half children who finish their secondary education each year, there is now room for only about 440,000 in institutes of higher education. Of these, only half can be admitted to regular daytime universities and institutes of technology. The rest must be content with night schools or correspondence courses.

For many years the Kremlin kept expanding the universities. But more recently the expansion has been drastically curtailed.

"We made a serious mistake in the past in turning out too many university-trained specialists," a Soviet educator has commented. "In our factories we don't need university graduates. We need foremen trained to read graphs and turn valves. From now on we shall send more young men to technical high schools, and fewer to the universities."

Needless to say, this educator was not suggesting cutting back the output of engineers and scientists needed to develop nuclear weapons, space rockets or new industrial machines. On the contrary, the Kremlin feels that it is for these persons that the universities should be primarily reserved.

THE majority of students in Soviet institutions of higher learning study the sciences rather than the Arts. Science students are favoured not only in the number of vacancies provided but also in the size of grants, and in the rewards awaiting them. A senior practising physician averages £70 a month, but a top scientist can earn £400 to £600 a month.

Furthermore, foreign students at Soviet universities have reported that teaching standards in the sciences are far superior to those in law, economics and similar subjects which are not considered so important by the Kremlin leaders. The Arts suffer a further disadvantage in that a dispassionate study of them involves repeated conflict with Communist political doctrines. But there is one Arts course which all university students must take each year. That is Marxism-Leninism, the study of Marxist doctrine. Every year students plough through the works of the two party prophets and attend lectures on the "science" of Marxism. Most of the students find the course a deadly bore.

Russia's rigid, old-fashioned system of education has recently come in for severe criticism by the Kremlin for its failure to prepare Soviet youngsters for adult life. The tremendous increase in the number of students seeking admission to universities, coupled with the country's current labour shortage, prompted Khrushchev in 1958 to denounce Soviet youth's reluctance to "soil their hands in physical labour" and to endorse some proposals for making education more practical.

One proposal advanced by Khrushchev was that all students should go to work for a period of time after completing their schooling. This met with such resistance from educators, parents and leading scientists that a much modified reform was instituted. Students are now to get more vocational instruction during school, and then upon taking their final examinations they must either interrupt their studies for two years, taking jobs in factories, or else work and study part time at evening or correspondence courses which cover a part of the university curriculum. Exceptionally gifted students, however, particularly in the sciences, will be allowed to enter a university or technical institute without interruption.

The new reforms are only gradually being put into effect, and how they will ultimately work out is a matter of speculation even for Soviet authorities. Asked whether the new programme would achieve its aims, the Soviet Minister of Higher Education once told a visitor: "Come back in three years and I'll tell you."

SCHOOLS, of course, perform only a part of the task of bringing up younger people. In most parts of the world parents and usually the Church play an equally important role. As noted in an earlier chapter, family life in the Soviet Union is severely restricted. But the Church's influence has suffered even more drastically.

Embracing the atheism of Marx, who had called religion the "opium of the people," the Communists have followed a militantly anti-religious policy. One reason is that the Orthodox Church was an especially baneful influence in czarist Russia. Another was the Communists' conviction that their party could tolerate no rival for the loyalty of its followers. Because the Church's teachings were so diametrically opposed to the Communists' materialistic philosophy, it was a potentially even more dangerous rival than opposition political parties.

From the beginning, therefore, the Soviet regime carried on a ruthless campaign of closing churches, arresting and exiling many priests and fostering a vigorous propaganda campaign against religious worship of all varieties. The campaign had a fair amount of success among young people, among urban intellectuals and among those who were forced by pressure to make peace with the regime. But the centuries-old hold of the Church was not entirely broken.

When the Germans attacked Russia in 1941, Stalin saw he must mobilize all possible forces to rally the country, and he sought to make peace with the Orthodox Church. He was aided by the readiness of the Church hierarchy to come to terms with the Communists. An agreement was presently reached between the Kremlin and the acting Patriarch of Russia whereby the Church was allowed to publish religious books and a Church magazine and to reopen its theological schools. The anti-religious propaganda campaign was relaxed. Other religious groups, including the Protestants, Moslems and Jews, were granted similar respites.

The easing of anti-religious oppression, coupled with the popular thirst for spiritual solace from the hardships of the war, fostered a limited religious revival in the Soviet Union. Churches were again crowded, while the priesthood for its part called upon the congregations to defend the country and support their atheistic ruler, Stalin, "with deep love and gratitude."

SINCE the war the Orthodox Church has continued to serve the Kremlin faithfully at home and abroad, and today it enjoys a measure of freedom to worship and safety from persecution. Other beliefs have fared less well. The Jews in particular have suffered periodic revivals of anti-Semitism, a phenomenon which in Russia had its antecedents under the czars.

For example, the passport which every Soviet citizen must carry specifies the bearer's "nationality." Because the Kremlin considers the Jews a nation every Jew is labelled, just as Hitler labelled non-Aryans in the Third Reich. The Jews also suffer severe disadvantages in the choice of a profession and in entrance into certain educational institutions. While it is probably an exaggeration to say that Jews in Russia today are persecuted, it is undoubtedly true that they are targets of systematic discrimination.

The religious revival which began during the war continues. A visitor to the Baptist church in Moscow—the only Protestant house of worship in the capital—will find it packed with perhaps 2,000 people crowded into a building designed for a few hundred. Even the temporary balconies are a sea of solemn, devout faces.

A closer look at any congregation in the Soviet Union, however, reveals that most of the worshippers are older people who were born and brought up before the Revolution, and nine out of ten of them are women. In provincial cities one may find a slightly larger proportion of young people. But to interpret this as a sign of a mass religious revival would be misleading. As the older generation dies off, religion is likely to become even less of a force in Soviet life.

DESPITE the combined efforts of Agitprop, the Pioneers and Komsomol, of the Soviet schools and universities and the Soviet family, Russia today has a "youth problem" similar to those of Western nations. While the problem does not by any means involve all Soviet youth, its symptoms are dramatically evident in a small but significant minority.

The juvenile delinquents of London and Glasgow have their counterparts in Russia in the so-called "hooligans," whose name the Communists imported from the West. The hooligans are particularly troublesome in the major cities. These gangs, who infest the parks, cinemas and sports stadiums, are a product of boredom and of a lack of respect for the older generation, aggravated by the disruption of family life. Frequently the police have proved powerless to cope with them.

Typical of the incidents that have occurred was one in Leningrad, where an outstanding student from Moscow University remonstrated with a gang of hooligans who were brawling in a public park. The hoodlums drew knives and stabbed the student to death.

These boys were subsequently apprehended, tried and shot. But similar outrages continued until authorities proposed that the party organize groups of vigilantes or auxiliary police to patrol the public parks and streets in groups of five or six, especially during holidays. The response was

immediate. Units were made up not only of party members but of non-party citizens.

In contrast to the hooligans, Russia's *stilyagi* ("style hounds") are more or less peaceable citizens. Like America's former zoot-suiters and the "teddy boys" of Britain, the *stilyagi* seem to be motivated chiefly by a desire to attract attention. Their method of self-expression is to wear odd clothes: tight trousers, strange hats and gaudy neckties. They can be seen in any restaurant that has an orchestra, even in Moscow's staid, ultra-conservative National Hotel.

THE *stilyagi* are not a real menace, but they are a disturbing indication of the ferment that has attacked Soviet youth. The great majority of young Russians are restless and unsatisfied with the world they are inheriting. They are indifferent to the Communist faith which their parents embraced, although they do have great pride in the Soviet Union as a nation.

But far more important, many young people are seeking the less material benefits of a civilized Western community: wider knowledge of contemporary art, music and literature, and the right to think and write and talk as they please. At times they have even openly questioned the party's propaganda efforts. Their restlessness at the time of the Hungarian revolt in 1956 led to stirrings and demonstrations within Moscow University, with such effect that Khrushchev himself felt compelled to go the great gleaming temple of learning on Lenin Hills and read the student body the riot act. Any further unauthorized demonstrations, said the First Secretary, would be severely punished.

The hooligans and the *stilyagi* may be temporary afflictions similar to those found in the younger generation of every modern country. But the discontent among the larger body of youth goes deeper. Though it is hardly likely to erupt into open defiance, it does demonstrate how the Communist party, with all its propaganda apparatus, has failed to create that long-promised hero—the New Soviet Man.       .

*Kissing the icon of St. Sergius, a woman venerates the patron saint of Russia at the monastery named after him near Moscow*

# Target: Mind and Soul

The minds of Russia's citizens are a continuing target for government persuasion. Thought control begins with State supervision of newspapers, books and films. Conformity is increased by State definitions of "correct" views on everything from art to zoology. While the officially atheistic State has found it too costly to extirpate religion, as the pictures on this and the next pages show, the Soviets turn the church to their purposes by making it inculcate patriotism. The Orthodox Church lends itself to this device as it has been historically responsive to secular authority.

THE CENTRE OF FAITH *for devout Russians for six*
*centuries has been the Monastery of the Holy Trinity and St. Sergius,*
*in Zagorsk, where Church tradition decrees an elaborate ritual*

AT COMMUNION in the Zagorsk Monastery of the Holy
Trinity and St. Sergius (*opposite*), a priest partakes of
wine before cutting the bread and placing it in the chalice.

PATRIARCH ALEXIS, the spiritual head of Russia's Orthodox Church, wears a cross-topped mitre while seated before the opened altar screen (*background*) at Zagorsk.

MEDICAL STUDENTS, men and women of Stalinabad, the capital of the Tadzhik Republic in Central Asia, attend a lecture beneath portraits of Lenin and Stalin. In this Moslem region, the Soviets have named the school the Avicenna Medical Institute, honouring the medieval Arab philosopher-physician who was born near Bukhara.

EDUCATION *in the Soviet Union is provided with an eye to strict discipline. In the universities it is organized primarily to fulfil the need for scientists and teachers*

RENOWNED PHYSICIST Lev D. Landau, who ranks as one of the world's leading theorists on the behaviour of matter at extremely low temperatures, teaches at the Institute of Physical Problems in Moscow. Great professors like Landau are usually given light teaching duties so that they may have more time to pursue their own research.

RAISING ARMS, children in a Moscow primary school imitate clouds and lightning as the teacher describes the weather. School uniforms, which were standard up until the Revolution, have been brought back again by the State gradually in the years since 1936.

WITH GIRL FRIENDS on the way to a science museum Alexei reads a Russian-English phrase book. In his English classes English is spoken more often than Russian.

TEENAGE STUDENT *Alexei Kutskov, in his last year at Moscow's School 49, spends six days a week on a heavy study programme that includes astronomy, sixth-year English, fifth-year physics*

AT THE PIANO Alexei plays a foxtrot for a school evening social. A conscientious musician, he practises for an hour every day.

PLAYING VOLLEYBALL, Alexei anxiously watches the ball as a team-mate stumbles. Volleyball is the No. 1 participant sport in Russia, and Alexei plays at one of Moscow's many athletic clubs.

IN CHEMISTRY LAB Alexei writes up a report. Education in the Soviet Union holds the key to personal advancement and Alexei studies diligently to enter a university and become a physicist.

THE LIFE OF YOUTH *is*
*strongly influenced by the*
*State. The government*
*provides daytime nursery schools*
*for the very young and*
*organizes a thoroughgoing*
*physical fitness programme*

DANCING, pre-school children whose parents
are employed in a gas works near Moscow pass
the day in a State-supported factory nursery.

CAMPING near Leningrad (*below*), Pioneers take part in a scouting exercise. Competitions were held in tent-pitching, hiking and cooking.

BROWSING. Students gather at a Moscow University bookstall. Tolstoy, Chekhov and Gorky sell very well, but the only foreign authors available are those whose works are approved by the State.

# The Thaw
# in Arts
# and Letters

AN old Russian legend tells of an impover-
ished Russian noblewoman who wanted to
refurbish her large, bare palace in St. Petersburg.
Unable to afford the usual marble statuary, she
had one of her handomest serf girls frozen in ice
and set up in the foyer of the palace.

Many observers maintain that during the rule
of Josef Stalin Russia's arts and literature, like the
serf girl, were frozen in ice. Though they are
still rigidly encased today, there are signs that the
ice is beginning to melt and that Soviet culture is
stirring restlessly in its frosty prison.

A widespread impression in the West has been
that Russian culture has existed only on the surface
of Russian life. This belief holds that artists and
writers have been deprived of influence on the
upper levels of power by the autocracy of both
the czars and Communists and that they have
been prevented until recently by the nation-wide
illiteracy from sinking their roots into the masses.

The impression is a false one. While it is true that Russian writers have failed to instigate a successful liberal political movement, their influence has been profound in the formation of liberal thought and in the enunciation of the national identity and purpose.

Despite the illiteracy of a past age, Russian authors have always enjoyed a large, avid and attentive audience and the Kremlin's mass education drive has further enlarged that audience. From the poetry of Pushkin to the great novels of Dostoevsky, Russian literature has been acclaimed throughout the world for generations. Nowhere today are books printed in such quantities as in the Soviet Union. Not merely contemporary popular literature but new editions of the great Russian classics, from Gogol to Gorky, are snapped up overnight. A new 20-volume edition of Tolstoy's collected works which will not be completed for at least five years has already had its entire edition of 700,000 copies sold out by advance subscriptions. In the Moscow underground one often finds half the passengers immersed not in newspapers or popular magazines but in worn tomes of Turgenev, Chekhov or Pushkin.

The enthusiasm for culture extends far beyond literature. In the whole U.S.S.R. there are 385 permanent repertory theatres and 32 opera companies. In addition, Moscow and other large cities are dotted with auditoriums, sometimes run down and unheated, but frequently filled to overflowing by audiences eagerly listening to readings of poetry or other Russian classics.

THE ballet is, of course, the supreme example of Russian achievement in the performing arts and its cathedral, Moscow's Bolshoi Theatre, seldom has an empty seat. The tradition is an old one, dating from the day in the late 18th century when Catherine the Great brought the Italian choreographer Angiolini to St. Petersburg to teach the imperial ballet. Ever since then the Bolshoi has been the pride of all Russians. Back in the days of the First Five-Year Plan, when Moscow's shops were all but empty, a foreign housewife showed a mail-order catalogue of American dresses to her peasant girl servant and asked her to choose a Christmas present for herself. The girl thumbed through the pages for a while, then pushed the book aside and said to her employer, "Couldn't you get me a ticket to the Bolshoi?"

Each year hundreds of children apply for admission to the Bolshoi's ballet school, but only 30 to 40 are accepted. For nine years the lucky ones take regular educational courses but they practise dancing assiduously at the same time. Then, in one final test given before the directors of the Bolshoi and other ballet companies of the country, their entire future fate is decided. The Bolshoi gets its choice of the best. Those it rejects are snapped up by the ballets in provincial capitals and there, in all probability, the dancers will spend the rest of their lives.

APART from literature and the performing arts, Russia has given the world some of its greatest musicians. Its contemporary composers include the late Sergei Prokofiev, who began his career before the Revolution, and Dmitry Shostakovich, who was born in 1906. They and others continued to write during Stalin's repressive era, although their works were frequently banned by his censors for failure to comply with his tastes. Today a number of young composers are experimenting with new forms of music, as are their contemporaries in the West.

The harnessing of all Russian culture to the Communist machine dates back almost to the Revolution. Lenin had said, "Socialist proletariat literature cannot be an instrument of gain for persons or groups; it cannot altogether be an individual matter, independent of the whole proletarian cause. Down with non-party writers!" In the 1920s, however, literary works were not severely censored; only avowedly anti-Communist writings were forbidden and a number of inventive writers made their appearance. The literary giant of this period was Vladimir Mayakovsky. In addition to his fine lyrical poetry, Mayakovsky turned out propagandistic doggerel for the party. But he also wrote stinging satires of the Soviet bureaucracy.

In the 1930s Stalin began to cut down on the

free expression of ideas. When the Union of Writers was founded in 1932, Stalin's disciplinarians used it to control the literary intelligentsia. All prominent writers had to join the Union.

The pressure was at first relatively mild. When Mikhail Bulgakov, a non-Communist writer and author of one of the few great post-revolutionary plays, *Days of the Turbins*, found his works being banned and his plays removed from the stage, he personally asked Stalin for permission to leave the country. As a writer, he said, he had no place on the Soviet scene. Stalin promptly denied his request. The regime, said Stalin, needed all the talents it had. Like a benign father he advised Bulgakov to adapt himself to the Soviet rules. Then he raised the ban on some of Bulgakov's works, appointed him assistant director of the Moscow Art Theatre—perhaps the greatest theatre in the world—and sent the playwright on his way unharmed.

But Stalin's benignity did not last long. As the terror grew and the purges gathered momentum, many writers went into obscurity or were shot. Eventually only the works of servile hacks and terror-stricken scribblers were published.

AS his power became absolute, Stalin extended his control over the entire cultural life of the country, imposing his own personal tastes on writers and composers. When Shostakovich's works displeased him he sent the young man off to Archangel in the far north for a few months, scolding him for his "formalism." In the late 1940s Shostakovich was again taken to task for writing "unharmonious, anti-democratic music," by which Stalin apparently meant his pieces did not have enough catchy tunes.

Stalin's precept for all creative art was called "Socialist realism." Still in force today, the precept has never been very clearly defined. Generally it means that only those themes which will contribute to the strengthening of Socialism should be dealt with. For example, writers are urged to describe how a Soviet factory exceeds its Five-Year Plan quota for producing steel, how a collective farm increases the size of a pig's litter or how border guard's vigilance thwarts capitalist sabo-

teurs from spreading boll weevils on a State cotton farm. Because complex love stories or themes involving the inner conflicts of individuals contribute nothing to the building of Socialism, they are frowned upon.

"Realism" applies to the way a story is told, a piece of music composed or a picture is painted. Music must be tuneful and it should preferably be based on folk themes and devoid of all the new techniques of contemporary Western music. All creative works must depict "Socialist truth"—in other words, life as the Kremlin would like it to be. Workers must be revealed as happy, their homes spacious, their farms clean and their lives gay.

In Soviet jargon the heroes of Socialist realism must be "positive," *i.e.*, noble prototypes of the New Soviet Man. Villains must be "negative," *i.e.*, altogether bad, with no endearing features that might tempt the reader to sympathize with those who deviate from the Soviet ideal. To demonstrate the superiority of the Socialist system, the hero must always win and the villain must be liquidated—or reformed.

The guardians of Socialist realism are the party-appointed officials of the government censor's office and the party hacks in the Writers' Union. They control not only all the literary critics but all the publishing houses. They cannot always monitor a writer's thoughts or prevent him from composing a poem or story contrary to the rules. But if he creates non-Socialist-realist compositions, they can and usually do prevent him from getting published.

EXCEPT for a brief wartime relaxation, Stalin's control over Russian writers continued unabated for 20 years. Especially severe was his treatment of Jewish writers, a number of whom, accused of "homeless cosmopolitanism" (*i.e.*, they were too sympathetic to Western ideas), disappeared without a trace. A few authors during this period stopped writing for publication altogether. Boris Pasternak, for example, withdrew from public life, devoting himself to poetry and fiction which he knew could not be published and earning his living by translating Shakespeare and other foreign classics into Russian. Other writers dutifully turned out the monotonous drivel to which Soviet literature had descended. But their resentment and their yearning for more latitude were not quenched. When Stalin died in 1953 they thought their hour had finally come.

At first a definite change seemed to have occurred. The new era began when one of Stalin's ablest literary sycophants, Ilya Ehrenburg, burst into print with a novelette entitled *The Thaw*, which gave this brief period its name. The book mentioned such taboos as the great purges of the 1930s and attacked official Soviet art as "philistine." The mere fact of the book's publication roused widespread hopes that Soviet literature was at last to be freed of its shackles.

For a period of almost three years Russia's best-known writers and poets published increasingly nonconformist work. One young novelist named Vladimir Dudintsev startled and thrilled the reading public with a novel provocatively called *Not by Bread Alone*, in which he openly attacked the hidebound captains of Soviet industry and critized highly placed government bureaucrats.

Criticism of the regime and, indirectly, of some aspects of the Communist faith itself grew, encouraged by and in turn encouraging the repressed writers of the satellite States, particularly those in Poland. The Kremlin's hacks in the Writers' Union grumbled, but they hesitated to retaliate.

THEN in the autumn of 1956 the anti-Soviet storm broke, first in Poland and afterwards in Hungary. Shocked that their literary colleagues in Warsaw and Budapest had taken advantage of the Kremlin's leniency to turn on the Russian State, most Russian writers meekly submitted to the control of the party hacks. But a handful of prominent writers demurred.

When they were called upon by the leaders of the Writers' Union to recant their sins, the rebels fell sullenly silent, refusing to go through the long-established Soviet ritual of confession. Khrushchev himself, incensed by what was termed the "campaign of silence," addressed a gathering of writers and urged the silent ones to repent. Some

did but still a few held out. It was the most daring defiance of the Kremlin since Stalin had come to power.

AT last Khrushchev summoned the leading authors to his *dacha*. There on the lawn he told them in unambiguous terms that the Kremlin would no longer tolerate their insubordination. If an outburst like the Hungarian writers rebellion were to occur in the Soviet Union, he said, he would repress it with force. "My hand would not tremble," he added ominously.

The recalcitrant writers were horrified that a new terror might begin, and one of them, Margarita Aliger, fainted dead away. Subsequently Aliger and a few of the rebels admitted their "errors," but so ambiguous were their confessions that there was considerable doubt as to their sincerity.

Meanwhile Boris Pasternak had completed and submitted to his publishers his now famous *Doctor Zhivago*, a complex novel that deals in part with a Russian intellectual's unenthusiastic reaction to the Communist Revolution. The book contained many sharp but indirect criticisms of the Soviet regime. While waiting for his Soviet publishers to make up their minds about the novel, Pasternak gave a copy of the manuscript to an Italian pro-Communist publisher, granting him permission to produce it abroad. Finally the Kremlin's censors rejected the work. When they discovered that it was about to be published in Italy, they sent the head of the Writers' Union personally to attempt to dissuade the publisher. But the publisher refused, and brought out the novel.

This in itself signalled trouble for Pasternak, but to make matters worse the novel won him the Nobel Prize for his life's work. The party watchdogs in the Union turned on him savagely but many of the Union's members refused to join in the attack and silently stood by the author. While the storm raged about him, Pasternak continued to live quietly at his country home near Moscow. Eventually the attacks on him subsided. In 1960 he died, still acknowledged as the greatest contemporary Russian poet by a host of Russian readers.

In other branches of art a similar though not so pronounced development has taken place. The great majority of contemporary dramas still cling drearily to the old conventions, but over the past few years a few new plays slightly transgressing the laws of Socialist realism have appeared on the stage. In painting, a handful of new men have experimented with abstract art, achieving no official acceptance but exciting the curiosity of the West. In music, young composers are writing material which they know cannot be performed under present rules but which seems to assuage their thirst for something new.

Only the ballet of the Bolshoi Theatre, the classical stronghold of Russian art, appears to remain firmly bogged down in Soviet conservatism. Year after year the same classical works and a few unimaginative new ballets are performed with ever more brilliant technical skill and gaudy scenery, but with less and less originality or inspiration.

WHAT has been the impact of these developments on the Soviet public and what is their implication for the future?

Among the upper middle classes the effect has probably been slight. Most factory managers or engineers have little time to worry about the problems of the creative artist. Nor are they aware of the low level to which cultural standards have fallen. Their tastes, like the factories they run, lag thirty or forty years behind those of their counterparts in the West. To some Russians the epitome of architectural splendour is the ornate skyscrapers rising on the Moscow skyline. In their homes the symbol of genteel elegance is the tub-shaped orange and mauve lampshade whose long silk tassels dangle over the dining room table.

But in Soviet cultural life there is another audience, younger in tastes though not necessarily in years. This audience includes elderly professors whose esthetic standards and tastes were already established when the Revolution broke out. But it also includes young students to whom current Soviet literature seems crass and stultified in com-parison to the 19th-century classics and the few Western books which they have managed to read. They know they cannot return to a bygone tradition. But why, they ask, can they not move forward in search of new forms, new ideas and new methods?

It was the young students and young writers who were most deeply stirred by the rumblings in Warsaw and Budapest and by the timid trans-gressions of Ehrenburg and Dudintsev. Their quest for the new is constantly demonstrated in their avid questioning of foreigners about Western literary developments. What are Western authors writing, they ask? What has become of Howard Fast, the former Communist once officially lionized in the Soviet Union but excommunicated since he broke with the party? And—as if to seek confirmation for their own low regard for Soviet culture—what does the West think of the contemporary Russian arts?

Like almost all Soviet citizens, these questioning youths are proud of their country and its scientific and economic progress. But as their material needs cease to preoccupy them, they search for greater latitude of self-expression in the world of ideas. Surreptitiously they exchange home-made recordings (often made on used X-ray plates) of Western jazz and manuscripts of forbidden literature.

THE senior party officials, ordinarily too busy to read, nevertheless are aware of the rum-blings among the new young intelligentsia. For the moment they seem confident that they can control the yearning for greater freedom without resort to Stalinist terror. When the recalcitrants go too far, Khrushchev lectures them, but otherwise he ignores them. "I don't like to read," he told them recently. "I like to talk."

But the questioning and searching go on. The serf girl is still frozen in her case of ice, but in the warmer atmosphere of the post-Stalin era the ice is melting slowly. If ever it cracks and the body emerges alive, it may well pose some perplexing problems for the old men in the Kremlin.

*A privileged composer, Aram Khachaturyan was criticized by*

RENOWNED POET. Boris Pasternak gardened at home near Moscow while controversy raged over his novel *Doctor Zhivago*, banned by the State. He died in 1960.

GREAT VIOLINIST. David Oistrakh gives a lesson in the Moscow Conservatory. Extremely popular in the Soviet Union, Oistrakh has also won critical acclaim in the West.

*the party in 1948 for composing "bourgeois music" but later regained favour. His symphonies and ballet scores have earned him a fortune*

# Heritage of a Proud Culture

The heritage of Russian culture is one of the richest in the world. During the Middle Ages a splendid religious art flourished in Kiev before succumbing to the Tatar invasion. Arts and letters received new impetus with Peter the Great's "Westernization" drive in the early 18th century, the movement culminating in a sudden blossoming a hundred years later. Russia's 19th century cultural renaissance began with the classical poetry of Pushkin. Then came the masterful novels of Dostoevsky, Turgenev and Tolstoy, the evocative plays of Chekhov and the romantic music of Tchaikovsky and Rachmaninov. Today, despite severe restraints, the tradition has been carried on by courageous artists and writers like those shown here.

CHURCH ART *shone above all other forms in old Russia because of the rich tradition which came to southern Russia from Byzantium almost a thousand years ago. The characteristic onion-shaped domes of Orthodox churches were developed by native architects in northern Russia*

GILDED DOMES of Our Saviour's Cathedral in Moscow are topped by elaborately-embellished crosses. The drums supporting the domes are decorated with coloured tiles.

LAVISH INTERIOR of Kiev's Cathedral of St. Vladimir (*opposite*) is rich in paintings. Built in the 19th century, St. Vladimir's was modelled after early Kievan churches.

A CLASH IN PAINTING *persists in the Soviet Union. The State wants "Socialist realism"—poster art for political propaganda. But young Russian painters want to express personal feelings and are trying abstractionism*

OFFICAŁ ART is typified by a canvas showing Lenin speaking during Bolshevik seizure of power in 1917. The painting, by V. A. Serov, is prominently displayed in a Moscow museum, where crowds throng past it.

PERSONAL ART in an extreme idiom is exemplified by the frenzied self-portrait of a young painter, Anatoly Zverev. The picture is kept in Zverev's closet. He has never exhibited in Russia and sells only to friends.

131

**PERFORMING ARTS** *are regimented on a huge scale by the Soviet Ministry of Culture, which uses them for indoctrination while appeasing the people's ravenous hunger for culture*

A POLITICAL "WESTERN" is filmed by a State film company: The film deals with "the coming of Soviet power to Kirgizia." The Bolsheviks are the heroes and their opponents are outlaws.

A "DECADENT" OPERETTA, "Sylva," by Imre Kallman, is put on in Moscow. Such light Viennese entertainment is extremely popular, and Soviet officialdom tolerates it.

TOP CULTURAL SHOWPLACE, Moscow's Bolshoi Theatre (*opposite*) is jammed by bureaucrats, officers and foreigners for an opera. Most Bolshoi performances sell out.

BALLET'S BEAUTY is at a peak during a Bolshoi performance of *Swan Lake*. One of the most noted ballet companies in the world, the Bolshoi troupe works hard to maintain a classical tradition of impeccable technique and dazzling spectacle typical of an early 20th-century style.

# Collective Joy for the Masses

A GENERATION ago, when the First Five-Year Plan was getting under way, the little town of Sochi on the Black Sea coastline consisted of a few run-down villas that had once belonged to the aristocracy, two or three third-rate hotels, a public restaurant and a public bathhouse. But on a hillside overlooking the sea the white walls of a big new sanatorium for the Red Army were rising among the scraggy pines. The sanatorium was a portent of Sochi's future as the leading resort town of the U.S.S.R.

Today for many miles on each side of the town the seashore is dotted with more than 50 pinnacled palaces of rest set in statue-studded parks. Most of the palaces affect the wedding cake architecture of Stalin's day but the newer ones exhibit the austere lines that have been developed under Khrushchev.

Along the sea front an asphalt promenade is crowded with strollers. The men are dressed in striped pyjamas, their wives in cotton smocks or housecoats. Like crowds in any health resort they appear bored to death. Occasionally they glance in the windows of shops that sell souvenirs. One shop advertising "spoken letters" enables holiday-makers to make recordings that extend greetings to their families at home. Another sells coloured glass vases. Several display rows of bottles of Soviet brandy and champagne.

A little knot of holiday-makers is huddled about a bench in the park by the sea. In the middle of the group is a chessboard, and while the rest watch as eagerly as any football crowd, two men hunch

### WORLD CHESS CHAMPIONS

| | | |
|---|---|---|
| 1921-27 | Jose R. Capablanca | Cuba |
| 1927-35 | Alexander A. Alekhine | France |
| 1935-37 | Max Euwe | Netherlands |
| 1937-46 | Alexander A. Alekhine | France |
| 1946-48 | (Vacant) | |
| 1948-57 | Mikhail Botvinnik | U.S.S.R. |
| 1957-58 | Vasily Smyslov | U.S.S.R. |
| 1958-60 | Mikhail Botvinnik | U.S.S.R. |
| 1960 | Mikhail Tal | U.S.S.R. |

RUSSIAN PREDOMINANCE in chess shows up in a list of champions. Alexander Alekhine, a member of the Russian aristocracy, became a French citizen in the 1920s.

over the board deep in concentration, oblivious of the spectators around them. Chess is one of Russia's favourite pastimes. It is classified as a sport, and at the annual international championship, which is usually held in Moscow, Russians almost invariably are the winners.

To the average Soviet factory worker the prices of the souvenirs on sale at Sochi would seem staggering, but Sochi's window-shoppers are not average. Most of them belong to the privileged Soviet upper middle class, but among them are also some lower middle-class skilled workers from the factories in the north who have been rewarded for exceeding their work quotas by being given a holiday by the seaside.

Still others are holiday-makers from far-off Siberia: engineers, geologists and technicians who are generally kept in their remote jobs for two years and then given six months' holiday. In the distant north country there are few ways of spending the extra money they have earned for working in the wilderness. Now their pockets are bulging with wads of cash they have saved for the great splurge. Like the prospectors of America's Far West a century ago who would burst into San Francisco after a year or two in the mountains, they are making up for the long months of boredom with a well-earned spree.

In the evenings they congregate in the numerous restaurants along the coast, where jazz bands blare out as modern a rhythm as the Soviet authorities permit. With a curt nod, the men invite the lady diners to dance and then, oblivious of the beat, hurl their partners enthusiastically about the floor, bumping into other dancers, slipping and occasionally falling, but enjoying it all heartily. When the music stops they wipe the sweat from their faces, give their partners a gentle push toward the tables where they found them and return to their own tables for another swig of brandy or champagne.

While they wear pyjamas during the daytime at Sochi, in the evening they usually don slacks, short-sleeved shirts and sandals. Most of them are living not in the gleaming white sanatoriums but in one of the several new hotels which are also operated by the State. Some stay in boarding-houses run by the townspeople.

THE occupants of the sanatoriums are principally there to convalesce from heart, nerve or kidney troubles or some other ailment. Others are there simply to rest. All follow rigid daily routines: early breakfasts, gentle walks, long rests and a daily bus ride to the sulphur baths near the shore, where they are given their treatments. They have an early supper and hear the call of "lights out" just when the Sochi restaurants are waking up for the night.

The standard cure at the sanatoriums lasts precisely 24 days, and the standard price is £65, about equal to two months' salary for most of the patients. In the case of poorer factory workers who are really in need of convalescence, however, the State-run trade union often pays half or more of the bill. Upper middle-class patients are expected to pay for themselves.

Along the coast south of Sochi the road leads between high, green-painted fences. Occasionally through an open gate·one catches a glimpse of a luxurious villa set among well-kept lawns and overlooking the sea. Here Russia's highest officials and richest citizens pass their summer holidays in sumptuous comfort and in strict isolation from the lower classes.

IN 1959 half a million lucky Soviet citizens spent their holidays on the sunny beaches of Sochi. Perhaps another million found logings in similar Black Sea resorts like Yalta. It was in Yalta that Czar Nicholas II built a summer palace which he and his family occupied only briefly, before the Revolution deprived him of his throne and his life. More recently Yalta gained fame as the site of a 1945 conference attended by Roosevelt, Churchill and Stalin.

It is unlikely that more than one per cent of the Soviet population enjoys the privilege of a holiday in one of these resorts. The ordinary peasant, of course, takes what leisure he can get during the long winter months when the fields are deep in snow and the cattle snug in the barn behind the hut. That is the time for rest on the collective farms, and for carving the gingerbread panels which decorate the little rural houses.

The great majority of urban workers spend their month's holiday at home or at odd jobs which they take to supplement their meagre incomes. Some of them vegetate in a rented room in some *dacha* in the country. But the young people—the most favoured group in all Russian society—are well provided with amusements on the athletic fields and in the stadiums which are the boast of every modern Russian city.

Even Stalin, who starved and harried his subjects, recognized the importance to the country of a sound, healthy youth. As early as the 1930s the urban youth were encouraged to join athletic clubs at school or in the universities, in the Pioneers or the Komsomol or in the factories. Today sports facilities in Soviet cities are fully as good as those in Western countries.

Each city contains numerous clubs where volleyball, soccer, athletics and gymnastics are organized and taught. In the long winters skating and cross-country skiing are favourite pastimes.

Potential athletes are quickly spotted by local coaches and trainers. If their talents warrant, they are usually transferred to special physical-culture institutes or to schools that specialize in athletic training. Though they are expected to continue their academic studies in these institutions, or to coach younger athletes if they have already completed their own education, they are given special facilities and all the time they need for training. If they reach the championship standard they are placed under the best trainers and coaches the country can provide.

IN pre-revolutionary Russia sport was the exclusive prerogative of the aristocracy and wealthy groups and consisted chiefly of hunting and horse racing. Except for such traditional children's games as lapta, which resembles baseball, the majority of people had no opportunity whatever to participate in sports. And so when athletic competitions on a mass basis were introduced after the Revolution, the participants were understandably unfamiliar with the concepts of good sportsmanship and fair play.

One of the first cross-country ski competitions in Russia was a race from Moscow to Leningrad. The skiers left Moscow cheered on by their partisans, and when days later they sloshed into Leningrad, crowds assembled to watch the spectacle. Then a week later, according to reports, an enterprising sports reporter discovered that many of the participants had boarded a train on the outskirts of Moscow and stayed on until they reached the outskirts of Leningrad, at which point they put on their skis again and raced into town.

Today, however, the ethics of good sportsmanship are drilled into young athletes. In the Olympics and in other international competitions Soviet athletes have generally demonstrated that, like sportsmen from the West, they can be good losers as well as good winners.

## Collective Joy for the Masses

The Soviet government has openly exploited the prowess of its athletes for the purposes of national prestige, and has avoided competition in sports where the chances of winning were small. But even this attitude has become less marked. Recently the chairman of the Soviet equestrian sports committee urged the holding of an international match race between American and Russian trotting-horses. "We know your trotters are much faster than ours," he said, "but we want to compete with you anyway."

THE most popular spectator sport in the Soviet Union today is Association Football, which occupies a position similar to that in Britain. Almost every provincial city has a team in either the "A" (major) or the "B" (minor) League, and in the larger towns there are often several clubs organized within factories, unions or even government Ministries. Thus the Torpedo Club belongs to the ZIL car factory and "Dynamo" is the club of the internal security forces. Each club has teams participating in a number of sports, but the most important is invariably the soccer team.

Although the Soviet authorities describe all athletes as amateurs, good soccer players enjoy many of the prerogatives that professionals do in the West. They are not bought and sold by their clubs, but they receive special privileges and high salaries and the organizations that ostensibly employ them seldom ask them actually to report to work.

The Russian soccer fan is also as ubiquitous as the traditional Western sports enthusiast—and just as demanding. In cities that have only one athletic club the team is often organized by the municipal authorities. "If our team doesn't do well," the mayor of Tashkent recently told a foreigner, "I'm in trouble."

A leading soccer player is as much of a hero among Soviet youth as he would be in Britain. In a Pioneer camp in the heart of Siberia a foreign visitor asked a small camper what he intended to be when he grew up: "An engineer," he said, "and a soccer player like Yanshin." Lev Yanshin is the Soviet Union's leading goalkeeper.

EVERY Soviet city has its theatres and cinemas, and every factory has a "Workers' Club," usually a drab reading room whose walls are covered with slogans appealing for greater output. Night clubs, however, have no place on the Soviet scene except as their function is performed by a few restaurants where the richer members of the community try to dispel the drabness of everyday life. In Moscow there are a dozen luxurious restaurants, each representing a region of Russia and offering the specialities of that area. The most luxurious and expensive of all, the Aragvi, serves shashlik and excellent Georgian wines. In the summertime a favourite place to dance is the roof of the Moskva Hotel, overlooking the Kremlin.

New Year's Eve is the great occasion for such establishments, and many of the capital's most prosperous citizens reserve seats (not tables) at their favourite restaurant weeks in advance. The Metropole Hotel is probably the most popular end-of-the-year gathering place. In a dining room reminiscent of an old glass-roofed railway station, a large dance band plays from a high stage while the cream of Soviet society dances around a fountain in the centre of the room. Tables are set with elaborate pre-revolutionary crystal brimming with Soviet champagne and ancient silver bowls filled with black caviar from Astrakhan.

But again, this is only for a tiny fraction of the population. The great majority can afford at best a modest banquet in their crowded rooms.

THE chief characteristic of Soviet government-subsidized leisure is collectivity. The child in the Pioneer Palace is taught to prefer group dancing to individual ballroom dancing. The young sportsman gets his exercise as part of a team in a club. Unless he belongs to the well-to-do upper middle class, even the Black Sea holidaymaker is likely to be a mere digit in the sanatorium collective, riding to and from his mud baths in a bus. Even the hunter or the fisherman can get a licence to shoot or fish only as a member of a group organized where he works. If he wants to go off on a hunting trip, his club allots him and his fellows a camping area to which they are taken in the club's bus or lorry.

The underlying reason for this collectivity is, of course, the Kremlin's aim of developing a society in which the group or community is the basic unit. Individuals and individuality are considered enemies of the ideal collective Communist society, and no effort is spared to press people into a conforming group in which personal tastes, like private property, are submerged and eventually, the State hopes, eradicated.

The average Russian has learned to accept this, and whether he wants to sing or climb mountains, plant trees or simply play chess he realizes he must join a party-supported club. But whether he prefers this to individual effort and private amusement is something else again.

A strong feeling of individuality is a marked characteristic of the ordinary Russian, who by tradition prefers the privacy of his family to any large social group. Despite the facilities which the government has provided for organized sport, one of the most popular Sunday pastimes for a family is taking the tramcar to the edge of town and walking through the birch and pine forests. They have a picnic, and when the sun starts to go down they go home, the parents exhausted and sunburned, the children swollen by bee stings and weeping, but in the food hamper a large assortment of those most beloved of all Russian treasures, mushrooms.

Even high officials seem to prefer the small private pleasures to the organized fun of the community. The chief planner of the Ukraine, a senior Communist, had lunch one Saturday with a foreigner in Kiev but excused himself early, explaining that he had to hurry out to the suburbs to tend his little garden plot.

PERHAPS the most coveted possession a Soviet citizen can have is a private car in which to make excursions into the countryside. But thus far the government has made no effort to satisfy this craving. Although plans have been drawn up for the mass production of cars, these schemes remain on paper, and according to Kremlin officials the manufacture of small family cars will not be significantly expanded for at least another decade. In the meantime the State hopes, no doubt, to develop a preference among the masses for bus-travel. But the prospects at present are not promising.

A young and ardent Communist interpreter who had accompanied a foreigner through the hygienic delights of a Sochi sanatorium was asked once whether he would not enjoy a cure there during his holiday.

"Not me!" he answered. "When I get a holiday I go off to a village with my wife just to be alone for a while."

# Planning
# for
# Mass Fun

*Young athletes end a physical culture show with*

HOLIDAY COSTUME of loose-fitting cotton pyjamas is worn by male visitors to the Black Sea resorts. The Russians consider shorts improper street wear, but bikinis are common on beaches.

COLLECTIVE FARM BAND plays for an attentive Ukraine gathering. The State encourages such activity for the purpose of entertaining the farmers during the quiet days between planting seasons.

Indefatigable planners, the Soviet Union's leaders not only supervise all the work habits of the people but even attempt to dictate the way they should spend their leisure hours. In 1959 the Kremlin established the Union of Sports Societies and Organizations of the U.S.S.R. in an effort to get more people interested in sports. The trade unions and Komsomol, which were to direct the programme, were given the goal of increasing participation from 20 million to 50 million people by 1965. Moreover, not content with world-wide triumphs in chess and in track and field events, the Kremlin ordered efforts to be made to overcome Soviet weaknesses in swimming, tennis, skating and downhill skiing.

One of the first tasks the union undertook was to expand the already extensive practice of public physical training exercises conducted every morning in factories, farms, villages and government offices throughout the Soviet Union.

*a scramble as water jets are turned on in Moscow's Dynamo Stadium. The State emphasizes mass gymnastics for youth*

INDIVIDUAL ACTIVITY *is still preferred*
*to the organized fun of the community. Boating, skating*
*and strolling in the parks help fill the hours*

DRIFTING. Two cheerful rowers take their ease at a resort. Rowing boats are one of the most popular attractions at the Gorky Park of Culture and Rest in Moscow.

GLIDING ALONG (*opposite*). Children take skating lessons in a Leningrad park near an old church. Russia's skating season lasts from early November to April.

HISTORICAL SIGHT-SEEING attracts a party of Russians to the two-room house (*above*) in the Georgian town of Gori, where Josef Stalin lived as a boy. Russians tour in great numbers.

LAZY FISHING preoccupies two solitary anglers perched above the Dnieper River. Fishing societies determine who may fish where and when.

CHESS AT TWILIGHT absorbs casually-clothed men (*below*) in the Park of Culture and Rest in Alma-Ata. The game is a national passion and the Russians produce world-champion masters.

SWIMMING-POOL FUN delights a schoolboy playing above a canal constructed for boating and bathing in Leningrad's Kamenny Ostrov Park.

**PASSION FOR SPORTS** *runs the whole year round. The State wants its athletes to beat the world—and it wants physical fitness for military and economic reasons, too. Athletes occupy an exalted position in Russian society similar to that of artists and scientists*

PRETTY ROWERS, Moscow girls prepare to go out in their eight-oared shell. Well-trained Russian women athletes have defeated their Western counterparts in many international encounters, including the Olympics.

WINTER SUN WORSHIPPERS, including women in startlingly brief bikinis, catch the sun in the Leningrad cold. They lean against the walls of the historic Peter-Paul Fortress, which shields them from the winter winds.

BASKETBALL PLAYERS stage a fast game in a corner of Kiev's Dynamo Stadium. Basketball became a national sport in Russia in the 1930s, but the real boom started after the second World War, and now, as Russians explain, "from Vladivostok to Leningrad, everybody plays." Touring abroad, some teams have beaten good American opponents.

GREAT SPORTS STADIUM (*above*) looms white and spectral by Moscow's river. Named after Lenin, it houses athletic events throughout the year, in all kinds of weather.

SUNDAY SKIERS (*below left*), the vanguard of the thousands who will turn out before the day is over, dot Moscow's Izmailovsky Park, one of many ski centres. Since

the Russo–Finnish War of 1940, in which the Finnish ski troops held off non-skiing Russians, the sport has won hundreds of thousands of fans wherever there is snow.

TOBOGGAN SLIDE in a "Russian Hills" park offers switch-back rides, and attracts skiers and strollers as well as sledge-riders. Lights permit the slide to be used at night.

A WORKER on the production line of an automotive tool factory in Kiev symbolizes the Soviet industrial potential, one of the major keys to the country's future.

# 10

# A

# Belligerent

# Neighbour

KARL MARX was still a student in 1835, when the well-known French historian, Alexis de Tocqueville, called the attention of the world to the rise of two great new nations. One of these was dedicated to freedom; the other was founded on servitude. "The conquests of the American are . . . gained by the ploughshare," he wrote, "those of the Russian by the sword."

Armed with a new ideology calling for world revolution, Russia today faces the West across a shrinking globe and devotes twice as much of its total production to armaments as does the United States. What prospect is there that the conflict can be settled without resort to war?

It was long a dogma of Marxism-Leninism that before the final victory of Communism could occur, war was inevitable. Stalin's successors, however, have repudiated this doctrine and have held that war is no longer inevitable. As Khrushchev said, "One cannot repeat what the great

Lenin said in completely different historical conditions without considering the concrete situation and the change in the balance of forces on a world scale."

If the Russians have indeed repudiated a basic tenet of their faith—and some of Khrushchev's menacing statements to the West might indicate otherwise—does this mean that the Soviet Union, faced with the prospect of nuclear destruction, is no longer prepared to risk war to accomplish the final defeat of capitalism?

ALONG its western frontier, thanks to Stalin's conquests, Russia today lies secure behind a barricade of satellite States. The Communist puppet regimes rule over sullen, unhappy nations who learned from the Hungarian rebellion that the West is not prepared to risk war for their liberation. Their only hope of salvation lies in the possibility that, with the development of intercontinental missiles, they may no longer be worth what it costs to hold them enslaved.

In the East, however, the Chinese Communists pose a more disturbing threat. Ruling a country that is overpopulated, underfed and possessed of only the beginnings of an industrial base, Mao Tse-tung and his comrades apparently believe that they have little more than excess population to lose in an all-out war. The rich rice fields and mines of south-east Asia offer a tempting solution for their immediate problems. Symptomatically, Chinese ideologists have disputed the Kremlin's assertion that war with the "imperialists" is no longer inevitable and have shown an alarming readiness to risk a conflict for the sake of southward expansion.

Bound to them by a common faith in Marx, the Kremlin leaders profess complete solidarity with their Chinese allies. One suspects, however, that they are less than enthusiastic about supporting a major Chinese thrust. As the Russian people become more vocal they are making it clear to the Kremlin that they want no war. More interested in better houses and more cars than in winning Asians to Communism, they are far from willing to make the sacrifices which military support of the Chinese would entail.

Beyond its ring of satellites and allies, Russia faces a world that is made up of two major blocs: a large number of neutral States politically uncommitted in the struggle between Moscow and the West, and Western-led alliances united to resist the Communist drive.

The Kremlin leaders have openly challenged the Western nations to compete economically rather than militarily for the loyalty of the neutral states. And they have already launched a costly campaign to woo the neutral countries through economic aid.

A visitor to the Stalingrad Tractor Factory, in which each day a hundred machines roll off the assembly lines, will notice that some are painted grey, some red. The grey ones are for home consumption. The red ones, which the factory engineers say are the best, are for export to the Middle East, India, Africa and south-east Asia, where the Kremlin hopes to gain a foothold by exploiting the new nations' impatience to modernize their economies.

In these areas the comparatively recent introduction of mass education, combined with envy of the rich nations of the world, has whetted appetites for a living standard which the local economies cannot now provide. If the West cannot persuade the new nations to pursue traditional democratic methods of development, they may well choose the more rapid methods of the Communists, and may do so despite the cost to them in civil liberties, whose virtues they have not yet learned to cherish.

WHAT are the Kremlin's objectives in regard to the Western alliance? No doubt the old party leaders believe that some day the Western nations will be isolated from the rest of the world and harassed by depressions and unemployment, and that the Western working classes will then rise and overthrow their "capitalist exploiters." Some Kremlin theorists believe that these nations, when faced with the superior might of the Soviet Union, will gradually surrender without a struggle.

For the immediate future the Kremlin's aims are more limited and more realistic. The leaders' avowed present aim is the stabilization of the status quo, keeping the balance of forces between the East and the West as it is. But they have one important reservation. To the Communists an essential element of the status quo is the continuous drive toward world Communism. Anything that impedes that drive is an attempt, they say, to alter the status quo, and therefore constitutes an act of aggression.

To Westerners this is obviously an absurd contradiction in terms, but the Communists, with their Alice-in-Wonderland logic, contend that since world revolution is inevitable, it must not be delayed.

The immediate realities of world politics, including American military strength, particularly in nuclear weapons, seem to have persuaded the Kremlin leaders that dangerous sources of conflict had best be settled by negotiation, at least for the time being.

But despite their readiness to talk about outstanding issues, they have no intention of missing any opportunity of harassing the free world, and they eagerly resort to angry threats and the crudest distortions whenever they see a chance to discredit the West in the eyes of the uncommitted nations.

While it woos the neutrals, the Kremlin still seeks to weaken the West, specifically the North Atlantic Treaty Organization. Eventually the U.S.S.R. doubtless hopes to force the withdrawal of Western troops from Europe and the elimination of their bases elsewhere in the world.

These, in brief, are the Soviet Union's chief aspirations abroad. But in the long run, the way the Kremlin solves the country's internal problems and responds to internal pressures will be equally important in determining the fate of the Communist movement abroad.

ONE of the Kremlin's most critical problems is that of adapting rigid Marxist principles to changing circumstances, for without adaptability to change no society or system can long survive. Just as Stalin's successors were willing to repudiate a basic tenet of Marxism-Leninism on the inevitability of war, it is not impossible that the Kremlin will scrap other major dogmas as Russia develops—perhaps even the militant doctrine of world revolution.

Closely allied to the doctrinal problem is the constitutional one: the selection and replacement of the dominant leaders in the Kremlin, and the role of the party and particularly of the Central Committee in this procedure. If the right of the Central Committee to choose between rivals is acknowledged, the authority of the winner and thus of the whole government is inevitably weakened. On the other hand, if no group is granted this power, the entire regime is constantly threatened with personal or political rivalries which at any time may bring about palace revolutions.

THE Kremlin leaders are also facing basic economic and social problems as the economy begins to emerge from one of scarcity to one of relative plenty. In the words of one Soviet specialist, these are "the problems at the end of the economic rainbow." In many ways they are similar to the problems which non-Communist countries in the West have been facing ever since they reached maturity.

They include the question of the distribution of wealth: how to prevent great accumulations of wealth and privilege on one side and lessen poverty and underprivilege on the other. They also include the problem of dividing the national production between private needs and public, between education and defence, cars and space vehicles—in brief the problem of feeding appetites that grow with eating.

The failure of the Communist system to produce changes vital to its functioning has created other problems as well. Thus far all the Kremlin's immense efforts through propaganda and political education to develop the "New Soviet Man" have failed. Far from being a selfless believer, free of old prejudices, eager to produce according to his abilities and satisfied with rewards that are measured only by his needs, the average young Russian today acts and thinks remarkably like his father and grandfather before him. If he is dedicated to anything it is to landing a good job with all the perquisites he can wangle—and preferably as far as possible from party headquarters.

Foreign observers of the Soviet Union have also noted a remarkable parallel between the development of Soviet society and that of quite different systems. As Thomas Mann described it in his novel *Buddenbrooks*, the first generation of a family—or a society—devotes itself to building economic power at all costs. The second generation takes its economic progress for granted and seeks social position—"to avoid soiling one's hands," as Khrushchev has complained. The third generation turns to cultural pursuits; perhaps a third generation in the Soviet Union will take economic power and position for granted, scorn the materialism on which Communism is based and search for rewards in the world of culture.

ONE of the most serious pressures confronting the Kremlin leaders is the yearning among intellectuals and youth for more latitude of self-expression. Writers are demanding that they be allowed to write what they really think about the real issues of Soviet life. And readers are avidly waiting for books that deal not with the building of Socialism but with the actual problems that confront them personally.

Though it is largely rejected by youth and evokes only lip-service among most members of the older generations, the Communist faith cannot be dismissed as a force in the Soviet Union. It is still the guiding doctrine of the Kremlin leaders who will be shaping Soviet policy for many years. Furthermore it constitutes a real attraction among the uneducated, underprivileged populations of the world. For this reason it will be a major force not only in guiding Soviet policy but in subverting the new nations for a considerable time to come.

Finally, there is another force, older and deeper, which plays a large role in the formation of Soviet policy today: Russian patriotism, which often borders on chauvinism. It is strong in the leaders, who are justifiably proud of their accomplishments in building the Soviet economy. It is strong among men in their forties and fifties who are proud of having defended their country against Hitler's invaders. It is strong among the intellectuals, who have been brought up in the tradition of Russian nationalism. It is perhaps weakest in the younger generation, who neither helped build modern Russia nor helped to defend it in the last war.

AS generations replace one another in the seats of power, how will these pressures and problems shape Soviet policies? In the absence of institutional procedures by which the top leadership can be replaced in an orderly manner, sudden changes of leadership and therefore of policy are always possible. At any time, supporters of the old Stalinist policies of rigid control and repression might resume power and reinstitute at least some of the old terror.

It is also possible, on the other hand, that proponents of a policy of greater relaxation—a policy designed to fulfill the aspirations of the younger generations and the universal longing for peace—might come to power. This might produce a less belligerent regime, more amenable to a truly peaceful co-existence based on mutual international respect instead of the sham now being trumpeted by the Kremlin.

Least likely, but also possible, is what Communists call "Bonapartism": the replacement of the party by the army as a means of control. Now that the power of the secret police has been curtailed, the army is the only force which could enforce a new discipline on the Russians in the name of national patriotism. If the army assumed such control, the marshals and generals might replace the dogma of "World Communism" with an equally dangerous one dedicated to "Moscow, the Third Rome."

In all events, while the challenge of Communism exists, there is no alternative policy for Russia's neighbours to pursue but the ancient formula: "If you want peace, prepare for war."

"Everything has happened in Russia," an old European ambassador with years of experience in Moscow once remarked. "And," he added, "anything is likely to happen again."

*On a summer evening couples dance on the Moskva Hotel roof overlooking the Kremlin. Next page: Moscow workers listen to a speech*

AS HOPES RISE *among the people for a more abundant future . . .*

*. . . new problems of adapting to change, of distributing wealth and*

*of allaying the individual's awakening curiosity confront the Kremlin*

# Appendix

## HISTORICAL DATES

862    Legendary founding of the Russian State: the people of Novgorod invite the Varangians, warrior-merchants from Scandinavia led by Rurik, to set up an orderly government. Start of Rurik dynasty

882    Varangians move south, capturing Kiev

c.990    Conversion of Russians to Christianity (Kievan ruler baptized in 988)

1019-54    Reign of Yaroslav the Wise. Kievan Russia attains peak of cultural and political development

1147    Founding of Moscow

1223    First Tatar invasion

1480    Overthrow of Tatar rule

1547    Ivan IV (the Terrible) crowned "Czar of All the Russias"

1556    Ivan the Terrible takes Astrakhan

1581    Ermak sets out for Siberia

1598    End of Rurik dynasty

1604-13    "Time of Troubles"

1613    Crowning of Michael begins the Romanov dynasty

1637    Russians reach the Pacific

1667    Russia obtains eastern Ukraine from Poland

1689    Russia's boundary with China fixed at the Amur River

1703    Founding of St. Petersburg by Peter the Great

1721    Peter acquires Estonia and Livonia from Sweden

1725    Establishment of the Academy of Sciences

1755    University of Moscow founded: first Russian university

1772-73    First and Second Partitions of Poland add Belorussia and most of western Ukraine

1773-75    Pugachev leads peasant revolt

1774    Russia obtains from Turkey the right to protect Christians under Turkish rule and to navigate the Black Sea

1784    First permanent Russian settlement in Alaska

1792    Catherine the Great acquires the Crimea from Turkey

1795    Third Partition of Poland adds Lithuania, Kurland and north-western Ukraine

1801-29    Russia annexes Georgia and part of Armenia

1809    Sweden cedes Finland to Russia

1812    Napoleon invades Russia

1815    Congress of Vienna awards Russia control of the Duchy of Warsaw

1825    Decembrist revolt

1855-56    Crimean War: Russia accepts neutralization of the Black Sea and loses the right to protect Turkey's Christians

1858-60    Alexander II annexes Pacific coastal lands. Founding of Vladivostok

1861    Emancipation of the serfs

1864    Local government and judiciary reforms

1864-84    Russia conquers western Turkestan and other Central Asian areas

1867    Russia sells Alaska to the U.S.

1881    Assassination of Alexander II

1892    Construction of the Trans-Siberian Railroad begins

1898    Founding of the Social Democratic party

1904-05    Russia defeated in the Russo-Japanese War

1905    The 1905 Revolution

1906    Meeting of the first Duma (parliament)

1914    Start of the first World War. Russia enters on the side of the Allies

1917    February Revolution forces the czar to abdicate. October Revolution brings Bolsheviks under Lenin to power

1918    Soviet Russia signs the Treaty of Brest-Litovsk ending participation in the first World War

1918-20    Civil war: counter-revolutionary and interventionist troops defeated

1919    Founding of the Communist International (Comintern)

1921    Introduction of the New Economic Policy

1924    Lenin s death

1927    Trotsky expelled from the Communist Party. Stalin supreme

| 1928-32 | First Five-Year Plan |
|---|---|
| 1929 | Intensive collectivization of farms begins |
| 1933 | United States recognizes the U.S.S.R. |
| 1933-37 | Second Five-Year Plan |
| 1936-38 | Stalin's purges |
| 1938 | Third Five-Year Plan begins |
| 1939 | Russia signs non-aggression pact with Germany. Second World War begins and Russia annexes eastern Poland. Russia invades Finland |
| 1940 | Russia annexes the Baltic states: Estonia, Latvia, Lithuania |
| 1941 | German invasion brings Russia into the War |
| 1943 | Comintern dissolved |
| 1945 | Second World War ends |

| 1946-50 | Fourth Five-Year Plan |
|---|---|
| 1948 | Communist coup in Czechoslovakia. Stalin breaks with Yugoslavia's Tito |
| 1948-49 | West Berlin blockaded by the Russians |
| 1950-53 | Korean War. Russia aids the North Koreans against United Nations forces |
| 1951-55 | Fifth Five-Year Plan |
| 1953 | Stalin's death |
| 1955 | Khrushchev effects reconciliation with Tito |
| 1956 | Sixth Five-Year Plan begins |
| 1956 | Poland's leadership changes. Hungary revolts |
| 1957 | Russia places first satellite in space |
| 1961 | Russia sends first man into orbit around the earth |
| 1959-65 | Seven-Year Plan |

# REPUBLICS OF THE U.S.S.R.

The U.S.S.R. is made up of 14 Soviet Socialist Republics and one much larger unit, the Russian Soviet Federated Socialist Republic. The Russian S.F.S.R. is subdivided into 13 Autonomous Soviet Socialist Republics, not listed here.

| | CAPITAL | POPULATION | AREA (sq. mi.) |
|---|---|---|---|
| Armenian S. S. R. | Erevan | 1,763,000 | 11,590 |
| Azerbaijan S. S. R. | Baku | 3,698,000 | 33,440 |
| Belorussian S. S. R. | Minsk | 8,055,000 | 80,150 |
| Estonian S. S. R. | Tallin | 1,197,000 | 17,410 |
| Georgian S. S. R. | Tbilisi | 4,044,000 | 26,910 |
| Kazakh S. S. R. | Alma-Ata | 9,310,000 | 1,064,090 |
| Kirgiz S. S. R. | Frunze | 2,066,000 | 76,640 |
| Latvian S. S. R. | Riga | 2,093,000 | 24,600 |
| Lithuanian S. S. R. | Vilnius | 2,711,000 | 25,170 |
| Moldavian S. S. R. | Kishinev | 2,885,000 | 13,010 |
| Russian S. F. S. R. | Moscow | 117,534,000 | 6,593,390 |
| Tadzhik S. S. R. | Stalinabad | 1,980,000 | 55,020 |
| Turkmen S. S. R. | Ashkhabad | 1,516,000 | 188,420 |
| Ukrainian S. S. R. | Kiev | 41,869,000 | 232,050 |
| Uzbek S. S. R. | Tashkent | 8,106,000 | 158,070 |

# Notes

## FAMOUS RUSSIAN CULTURAL FIGURES AND THEIR PRINCIPAL WORKS

### LITERATURE

| | | |
|---|---|---|
| Pushkin, Alexander | 1799–1837 | *Eugene Onegin, Boris Godunov* |
| Gogol, Nikolai | 1809–1852 | *Dead Souls, The Inspector General* |
| Turgenev, Ivan | 1818–1883 | *Fathers and Sons, A Sportsman's Sketches* |
| Dostoevsky, Feodor | 1821–1881 | *Crime and Punishment, The Idiot, The Possessed, The Brothers Karamazov* |
| Tolstoy, Leo | 1828–1910 | *Anna Karenina, War and Peace* |
| Chekhov, Anton | 1860–1904 | *The Cherry Orchard, Uncle Vanya, The Three Sisters, The Sea Gull, Short Stories* |
| Gorky, Maxim | 1868–1936 | *My Childhood, Mother, The Lower Depths* |
| Pasternak, Boris | 1890–1960 | *Doctor Zhivago, Selected Poems* |
| Sholokhov, Mikhail | 1905– | *And Quiet Flows the Don, Virgin Soil Upturned* |

### FINE ARTS

| | | |
|---|---|---|
| Rublev, Alexander | c.1370–1430 | Iconography: *The Trinity* |
| Bryullov, Karl | 1799–1852 | Painting: *The Last Day of Pompeii* |
| Repin, Ilya | 1844–1930 | Painting: *Zaporozhe Cossacks Drafting a Reply to the Turkish Sultan* |
| Fabergé, Carl | 1846–1920 | Jewellery: enamelled Easter eggs, jewelled birds and animals |
| Kandinsky, Vasily | 1866–1944 | Painting: abstractionism |
| Chagall, Marc | 1889– | Painting: expressionism |

## FOR FURTHER READING: A SHORT BIBLIOGRAPHY

### CHAPTERS 1, 2: LAND, PEOPLE, HISTORY

Carr, E. H., *A History of Soviet Russia.* 5 volumes. Macmillan, 1950–1959, 211s.

Charques, R. D., *A Short History of Russia.* Phoenix House, 1956, 21s.

Crankshaw, Edward, *Khrushchev's Russia.* Penguin Books, 1959, 2s 6d.

Hunt, R. N. Carew, *The Theory and Practice of Communism.* Geoffrey Bles, revised 1957, 18s.

Kennan, George F., *Soviet Foreign Policy,* 1917–1941. Van Nostrand, 1960, 9s 6d (Anvil Books).

Mirsky, Prince D. S., *Russia: Social History.* Cresset Press, revised 1953, 50s. Illustrated.

Moorehead, Alan, *The Russian Revolution.* Collins and Hamish Hamilton, 1958, 8s 6d.

Nollau, Günther, *International Communism and World Revolution: History and Methods.* Hollis and Carter, 1961, 35s.

Pares, Bernard, *A History of Russia.* Jonathan Cape, revised and enlarged 1955, 42s.

Rauch, Georg Von, *A History of Soviet Russia.* Stevens, revised 1960, 50s (Atlantic Books).

Seton-Watson, Hugh, *The Decline of Imperial Russia.* Methuen, 1956, 36s.

Sumner, B. H., *A Survey of Russian History.* Methuen, 1961, 12s 6d.

Utechin, S. V., *Everyman's Concise Encyclopaedia of Russia.* Dent, 1961, 30s. Illustrated.

Venturi, Franco, *Roots of Revolution.* Translated from the Italian. Weidenfeld and Nicolson, 1960, 63s.

Wolfe, Bertram D., *Three Who Made a Revolution: a biographical history.* Thames and Hudson, 1948, 30s. Illustrated

### CHAPTER 3: POLITICS

Bauer, Raymond and two others, *How the Soviet System Works.* (Harvard) Oxford University Press, 1956, 42s.

Fainsod, Merle, *How Russia is Ruled.* (Harvard) Oxford University Press, 1953, 68s.

Salisbury, Harrison, *Stalin's Russia and After.* Macmillan, 1955, 21s.

Schapiro, Leonard, *The Communist Party of the Soviet Union.* Eyre and Spottiswoode, 1960, 63s.

Scott, J. D. R., *Russian Political Institutions.* Allen and Unwin, 1958, 21s (cloth); 16s (paperback) (Minerva Series of Students Handbooks).

### CHAPTER 4: ECONOMY

Baransky, Nikolai N., *Economic Geography of the U.S.S.R.* Translated by S. Belsky. (Moscow Foreign Languages Publishing House) Lawrence and Wishart, 1957, 8s.

## MUSIC

| | | |
|---|---|---|
| Borodin, Alexander | 1833-1887 | *In the Steppes of Central Asia, Prince Igor* |
| Moussorgsky, Modeste | 1839-1881 | *Boris Godunov, Pictures at an Exhibition, Night on Bald Mountain* |
| Tchaikovsky, Peter | 1840-1893 | *Symphonies Nos. 4, 5, 6; Piano Concerto No. 1, Nutcracker Suite, Swan Lake* |
| Rimsky-Korsakov, Nikolai | 1844-1908 | *Scheherazade, Le Coq d'Or* |
| Rachmaninov, Sergei | 1873-1943 | *Piano Concerto No. 2, Symphony No. 2, Prelude in C Sharp Minor* |
| Stravinsky, Igor | 1882- | *The Fire Bird, Petrouchka, The Rite of Spring* |
| Prokofiev, Sergei | 1891-1953 | *Peter and the Wolf, Classical Symphony* |
| Khachaturyan, Aram | 1903- | *Masquerade, Gayne* |
| Shostakovich, Dmitry | 1906- | *Symphonies Nos. 1, 5, 7; Golden Age Ballet, Lady Macbeth of Mzensk* |

## PERFORMING ARTS

| | | |
|---|---|---|
| Stanislavsky, Constantine | 1863-1938 | Co-founder of the Moscow Art Theatre, innovator of "method" school of acting |
| Chaliapin, Feodor | 1873-1938 | Operatic basso who was outstanding in *Boris Godunov* and *Mefistofele* |
| Pavlova, Anna | 1882-1931 | Prima ballerina famous as *The Dying Swan* |
| Nijinsky, Vaslav | 1890-1950 | Premier danseur who was the first to dance *The Afternoon of a Faun* |
| Oistrakh, David | 1908- | Concert violinist |
| Ulanova, Galina | 1910- | Prima ballerina of the Bolshoi Ballet, outstanding in *Swan Lake* |
| Richter, Svyatoslav | 1914- | Concert pianist |
| Gilels, Emil | 1916- | Concert pianist |

Berliner, Joseph S., *Factory and Manager in the U.S.S.R.* (Harvard) Oxford University Press, 1957, 60s.

Dobb, Maurice H., *Soviet Economic Development Since 1917.* Routledge, revised 1951, 30s.

Granick, David, *The Red Executive: a Study of the Organisation Man in Russian Industry.* Macmillan, 1960, 21s.

Nove, Alec, *The Soviet Economy: an introduction.* Allen and Unwin, 1961, 25s (cloth); 15s (paperback) (Minerva Series of Students' Handbooks).

### CHAPTER 5: AGRICULTURE

Belov, Fedor, *History of a Collective Farm.* Routledge, 1956, 21s (International Library of Sociology).

Jasny, Navm, *Socialised Agriculture of the U.S.S.R.: Plans and Performance.* Oxford University Press, 1949, 60s.

### CHAPTERS 6, 9: LIVING CONDITIONS, LEISURE

Bauer, Raymond A., *Nine Soviet Portraits.* Wiley, 1955, 32s.

Hingley, Ronald, *Under Soviet Skins.* Hamish Hamilton, 1961, 21s.

Inkeles, Alex and Raymond A. Bauer, *The Soviet Citizen: Daily Life in a Totalitarian Society.* (Harvard) Oxford University Press, 1959, 50s.

Levine, Irving R., *The Real Russia.* W. H. Allen, 1959, 30s.

Lovell, Maurice, *The Soviet Way of Life.* Methuen, 1948, 4s 6d (Home Study Books).

Miller, Jacob, *Soviet Russia: an introduction.* Hutchinson, 1955, 10s 6d (University Library).

Miller, Wright, *Russians As People.* Phoenix House, 1960, 25s.

Salisbury, Marion, *To Moscow and Beyond.* Michael Joseph, 1960, 25s.

Werth, Alexander, *The Khrushchev Phase.* Hale, 1961, 25s.

### CHAPTER 7: EDUCATION AND RELIGION

Bereday, G. Z. F. and J. A. Lauwery (editors), *The Politics of Soviet Education.* Stevens, 1960, 45s (Atlantic Books).

Kline, George L. (editor), *Soviet Education.* Routledge, 1957, 21s.

Meek, Dorothea L., *Soviet Youth: Some Achievements and Problems.* Routledge, 1957, 28s.

Spinka, Matthew, *The Church in Soviet Russia.* Oxford University Press, 1956, 22s 6d.

### CHAPTER 8: ARTS AND LETTERS

Bowers, Faubion, *Entertainment in Russia: Ballet, Theatre, and Entertainment in Russia Today.* Nelson, 1959, 42s.

Gibian, George, *Interval of Freedom: Soviet Literature During the Thaw, 1954-1957.* (Minnesota) Oxford University Press, 1960, 34s.

Gorchakov, Nikolai A., *The Theatre in Soviet Russia.* (Columbia) Oxford University Press, 1957, 50s.

Hamilton, George Heard, *The Art and Architecture of Russia.* Penguin Books, 1954, 42s (The Pelican History of Art).

Hare, Richard, *Russian Literature From Pushkin to the Present Day.* Methuen, 1947, 4s 6d (Home Study Books).

Mirsky, Prince D. S., *A History of Russian Literature* Edited and revised by Francis J. Whitfield. Routledge, 1949, 40s.

Mirsky, Prince D. S., *Modern Russian Literature*. Oxford University Press, 1925, 6s (World's Manuals).

Simmons, Ernest J. (editor), *Through the Glass of Soviet Literature: Views of Russian Society*. (Columbia) Oxford University Press, 1953, 36s.

Slonim, Marc, *Modern Russian Literature: from Chekhov to the Present*. Oxford University Press, 1953, 55s.

Slonim, Marc, *An Outline of Russian Literature*. Oxford University Press, 1958, 8s 6d (Home University Library).

## Chapter 10: Trends

Boorman, Howard L. and three others, *Moscow-Peking Axis: Strengths and Strains*. Oxford University Press, 1957, 28s.

Dallin, Alexander (editor), *Soviet Conduct in World Affairs: a Selection of Readings*. (Columbia) Oxford University Press, 1960, 36s.

Dallin, David J., *The Changing World of Soviet Russia*. (Yale) Oxford University Press, 1956, 40s.

Dinerstein, Herbert S., *War and the Soviet Union: Nuclear Weapons and the Revolution in Soviet Military and Political Thinking*. Stevens, 1959, 37s 6d (Atlantic Books).

Fischer, Louis, *Russia Revisited*. Jonathan Cape, 1957, 25s. Illustrated.

Gunther, John, *Inside Russia Today*. Hamish Hamilton, 1958, 25s.

Harriman, Averell, *Peace With Russia?* Victor Gollancz, 1960, 12s 6d.

Kennan, George F., *Russia and the West Under Lenin and Stalin*. Hutchinson, 1961, 50s.

Roberts, Henry L., *Russia and America: Dangers and Prospects*. (Royal Institute of International Affairs) Oxford University Press, 1956, 25s.

Simmons, Ernest J. (ed.), *Continuity and Change in Russian and Soviet Thought*. (Harvard) Oxford University Press, 1955. 60s.

# Index

*This symbol in front of a page number indicates a photograph or painting of the subject mentioned*